Name:

Kid in the Middle

Consonant Digraphs

Blends

A Structured and Systematic Phonetic Reading Program

ReadBright Director: Sara Gross, M.S.Ed.
Educational Consultant/
Reading Specialist

Director's Assistant: Rochel Brenner

Program Authors: Sara Gross, M.S.Ed.

Dina Sobel, M.S.Ed.
Reading Specialist

Hannah Banker, M.S.Ed.
Reading Specialist

Editors: Michele Lyons, M.A.
Shira Felendler, M.S.Ed.

Contributors: Esther Malka Guzik
Gitty Perlberger
Devora Leah Lieberman
Malky Twerski

Graphic Artists: Rochel Brenner
Raizy Flamm
Miriam Weinberg
Adina Munk

Contributing Artists: Miriam Tova Leff
Antura Majdumer
Roy A. Wibowo
C. Beldean
Nilesh Patel

Images: © Shutterstock

Proofreaders: Mollie Rose
Dovi Stern
Chava Friedman

ISBN: 978-1-940205-63-2

FIRST EDITION
First Impression 2015
Second Impression 2017
Third Impression 2019
Fourth Impression 2022
Fifth Impression 2023

ReadBright

© ReadBright® 2015
All rights reserved

No part of this material shall be reproduced or transmitted in any form or by any means, electronic or mechanical, including photocopying without written permission from the publisher.

Printed in USA

732.569.0699
read@readbright.com
www.readbright.com

Note to Teachers:

ABOUT THE FOUNDER

The ReadBright program was developed by Mrs. Sara Gross, a nationally renowned reading specialist and educational consultant. She earned a M.S.Ed from Fordham University, and has amassed over thirty years of experience in the field of reading education. It is through the ReadBright program that Sara Gross makes her valuable materials available to other teachers. Her program has been successfully implemented in both general and remedial classrooms, and in small group and one-on-one settings.

THE SCIENCE OF READING

ReadBright is a highly effective, tried-and-true, structured literacy program for beginning readers. It is aligned with the latest cutting-edge research in the science of reading. The program incorporates phonemic awareness, phonics, vocabulary, fluency, and comprehension. All instruction is explicit, systematic, cumulative, multimodal, and data-driven. Moreover, this program is kid-friendly, eye-appealing and fun, so that teachers can maximize success in their classrooms.

WORD CLASSIFICATION

The ReadBright program presents phonics in a manner which is seamless and logical to a child. Students using the ReadBright program are trained to classify words into three main categories:
1. Kid in the Middle Words: cvc words
2. Magic e Words: cvc-e words
3. SpeedySpotter Words: words with vowel combinations and diphthongs

Each of these creative names depicts a mnemonic intended to aid students in word attack. Students using the ReadBright program are taught to classify words they encounter by identifying phonetic rules within the word. Students are empowered to identify appropriate word attack strategies once they are shown how to discern phonetic categories within a word.

READBRIGHT SCOPE AND SEQUENCE

The ReadBright Program incorporates the basic phonics rules over the course of three workbooks.
- **Book 1:** *Kid in the Middle* (CVC) words
  Consonant Digraphs (sh, ch...)
  Blends (cl, br, sk, mp...)
- **Book 2:** *Magic e* (CVC-E) words
  Walking Talking Vowels (vowel teams: ee, ea, ey...)
- **Book 3:** *Ruling R* (r-controlled vowels: ar, or, ir, ur, er)
  More Sounds (ou, oy...)

INSIDE EACH WORKBOOK:

Each workbook contains three sections: Phonics Rules, High Frequency Words, and Special Rules

A) PHONICS RULES

Phonics Rules dictate how a word should be sounded out according to its phonemes. In this book, phonics rules are presented individually in a clear and meaningful fashion. All skills are cumulatively reviewed as new skills are introduced.

Each page in the program is marked with an icon in the corner: *Read, Write, ☺ Activity, or Review.*

The following four worksheets are presented each time a new phonics rule is introduced:

1. **READ:** Reading Words. The initial exercise for each phonics rule is the Reading Words page, a page consisting of practice words with the new skill. This exercise is designed to help students gain familiarity with the new phonics rule.

2. **WRITE:** Mark the Word. This activity encourages students to notice applied phonics rules within words. In these worksheets, students are taught individualized markings to classify each phonics rule. They are then trained to mark up words in the correct fashion by utilizing these markings. The philosophy underlying this activity is this: Students who are instructed to discern categories of words are thereby empowered to identify appropriate word attack strategies while reading. Some Mark the Word pages provide practice of the skills using both real and nonsense words. Reading nonsense words ensures that students are truly sounding out the words rather than reading them by sight. This enables them to tackle any unfamiliar words they may encounter.

3. **READ:** Pyramid Reading. Targeted toward building reading confidence, these exercises will kindle students' enthusiasm to keep on reading. With its sequential, phonics-based layout, each pyramid strategically facilitates both reading fluency and accuracy. In the first book, high frequency words are bolded to make them easier for students to recognize. By reading pyramids, students will transition from the reading of isolated words to the reading of real text.

4. ☺: **Activity Pages**: These pages provide students with the opportunity to apply rules they have learned in a productive way.

B) HIGH FREQUENCY WORDS (known as POP WORDS in the ReadBright program):

High Frequency words are words that come up often in text. These are words that students learn to read on an automatic level. There are two kinds of high frequency words.

1. **Regular High Frequency Words:**
   - These are high frequency words which can be completely sounded out phonetically.
   - Example: *and*
   - These high frequency words are addressed through the teaching of the phonics skills in the program.

2. **Irregular High Frequency Words**
   - These are high frequency words which either cannot be sounded out at all or can only be partially sound out phonetically.
   - Example: *said, of*
   - Three to four irregular high frequency words are introduced in each unit.
   - These high frequency words are referred to as pop words in the ReadBright program.
   ○ Pop Words also include words for which students have not yet learned the phonics rule for sounding out that word.
   ○ Students are taught that these are important words that should "pop" out at them when reading. Students will learn to recognize these pop words quickly, and the words should "pop" out of their mouth quickly when they encounter them. The pop words include the most common high frequency words proven necessary for beginning reading.
   ○ For additional pop word practice, use the ReadBright pop word flashcards.

The following three sheets appear each time a new group of pop words is introduced.

1. **READ:** Reading Drill Sheet. This page presents pop words in isolation. Have students say and spell each word and then circle the words with their finger as they read them. On the last day of the week, they can use a pencil or crayon to circle the words as they read them.

2. **READ:** Repeated Sentences, Chants, or Poems. This page practices the new pop words of the unit. Each set of pop words that are introduced has a reading page practicing the newly taught phonics skill along with the new pop words. The targeted phonics skill and pop words are written on top of each of these pages. Each new pop word is repeated three to four times on the page. As the books advance in levels, the reading pages advance in difficulty as well. If necessary, read the sentences, chants and poems to students before having them read. These pages can be reread for an entire week so that children can develop accuracy and fluency with targeted phonics skill and high frequency words.

- BOOK 1:
  In the Kid in the Middle and Consonant Digraphs sections: Pop words appear in REPEATED SENTENCES. There are four sentences per pop word, where the pop word remains in the same place with only one or two phonetic words changing.
  In the Blends section: Pop words appear in CHANTS. The first three lines are the same and a rhyming line at the end of the chant is different.
- BOOK 2: Pop words appear in POEMS for advanced readers and REPEATED SENTENCES for weaker readers.
- BOOK 3: Pop words appear in READ AND RHYME POEMS. These are fun and exciting poems that can be read as a paired or choral reading.

3. ☺: **Activity Pages**: These feature new pop words.

Review: After each new skill is introduced, the reading and activity pages include previously learned phonics rules and pop words to provide cumulative practice.

C) SPECIAL RULES:

The end of each section features special rules for reading and spelling. The English language is replete with detailed phonetic rules. However, there are some exceptions to those rules. The special rules sections feature words that don't fit into a specific category or that simply follow a pattern of their own. These exceptions, however, are integral for shaping students' word attack skills and must be addressed. These skills are clearly explained and presented in the special rules section.

…AND FOR STRUGGLING READERS:

This program is designed for use by both general and special education classes. Here are some ideas to supplement and modify the program for struggling readers:

- Have students tap one of their hands on their desks while reading phonetic words, making one tap for each sound.
- Use clay or Wikki Sticks® to spell out pop words and to give these words a tactile dimension.
- Slow the teaching pace for pop words by reducing the quantity taught in a given week. However, keep the phonetic skills and sounds moving. Flip back in the book to introduce and review pop words while staying cognizant of students' ability and progress.

contents

page:

7	**ABC Review**		131	**Consonant Digraphs**
15	intro to reading			
19	**Kid in the Middle**		133	**ck**
21	*a*		138	pop words
30	pop words		141	**sh**
33	*i*		146	s/sh
42	review: *a • i*		148	pop words
45	pop words		151	**th**
48	*o*		156	t/th
58	review: *a • i • o*		158	review: *ck • sh • th*
61	pop words		160	pop words
64	*u*		163	**ch**
73	review: *a • i • o • u*		168	c/ch
76	pop words		170	sh/ch
79	*e*		171	review: *ck • sh • th • ch*
88	a/e		173	pop words
90	review: *a • i • o • u • e*		176	**wh**
96	pop words		178	pop words
99	**Special Rules**		181	**qu**
101	*s* (/s/ or /z/)		185	review: Digraphs
102	**Suffix *s***		190	pop words
109	pop words		193	**Special Rules**
112	**Double Letters**		195	. ?
122	pop words		197	!
125	**all**		199	,
128	*c* or *k:* Spelling Rule		200	" "
			202	**'s**

contents

page:
- **205 Blends**
  - 207 **Beginning Blends**
  - 224 *dr • tr*
  - 230 pop words
  - 233 **End Blends**
  - 243 **Beginning & End Blends**
  - 249 Triple-Letter Blends
  - 250 pop words
- **253 Sticky Sounds**
  - 254 ***ing • ink***
  - 257 ***ung • unk***
  - 260 ***ang • ank***
  - 263 ***onk • ong***
  - 265 review: Sticky Sounds
  - 269 pop words Colors
- **275 Special Rules**
  - 277 **Twin Letters**
  - 279 **Compound Words**
  - 286 pop words
  - 289 **Suffix *ing***
  - 293 **Suffix *ing:*** Spelling Rule
  - 296 pop words
  - 299 **Suffix *ed***
  - 309 **Suffix *ed:*** Spelling Rule
  - 312 pop words
  - 315 ***k*** or ***ck:*** Spelling Rule

Explanation of Symbols & Terms

/ /	A letter between two slashes indicates that the sound of the letter should be articulated rather than the name of the letter.
˘	˘ over a vowel indicates a short vowel sound.
¯	¯ over a vowel indicates a long vowel sound.
base (root) word	A base (root) word is a word that can stand alone as a word or have something added to it.
suffix	A suffix is a letter or group of letters that is added to the end of a word to change its meaning or form a different word.
syllable	Syllables are units of sounds which, when pronounced one after another, form a complete word.

Teaching Tip:

Introduce the following facts to students to help them better understand the basics of reading:

- There are 26 letters in the alphabet (abc).
- The alphabet is made up of consonants and vowels.
- There are 5 vowels: a, e, i, o, and u.
    (Sometimes y is a vowel, too.)
- All the other letters are called consonants.

- Consonants and vowels make up words.
    Every word has at least one vowel.
- Words make up sentences.
- Sentences make up stories.

- Letters come in pairs: capital and lowercase.
- Usually, lowercase letters are used.
- Capital letters are used at the beginning of a name or place, and at the beginning of a sentence.

ABC Review

Point to each pair of letters and say their name.

Aa	Bb	Cc	Dd
Ee	Ff	Gg	Hh
Ii	Jj	Kk	Ll
Mm	Nn	Oo	Pp
Qq	Rr	Ss	Tt
Uu	Vv	Ww	Xx
	Yy	Zz	

Vowel Review

Say the name and sound of each vowel.

1. Aa Ee Ii Oo Uu
2. e   u   i   a
3. o   a   u   o
4. i   e   a   i

5. Aa Ee Ii Oo Uu
6. a   u   e   a
7. i   o   a   u

ABC Review

1. Say the name and sound of each letter.
2. Circle the vowels.

1. D   I   M   B

2. R   Z   K   U

3. O   S   C   G

4. X   E   Q   N

5. J   T   H   W

6. Y   L   V   P

7.   A   F

ABC Review

1. Say the name of each letter.
2. Circle the vowels.

1. g   r   c   n

2. w   m   h   a

3. t   f   q   l

4. b   j   y   u

5. z   p   e   x

6. v   s   i   k

7.   d   o

ABC Review

1. Say the sound of each letter.
2. Circle the vowels.

1. j   y   f   o
2. n   h   b   e
3. q   i   r   l
4. g   c   w   t
5. z   s   u   a
6. p   k   d   v
7.   x   m

ABC Review

Say the name of each letter.

1. a a | g g | q q | t t | u u

2. q   a   t   g

3. u   q   g   a

4. g   t   u   q

5. t   g   a   t

6. u

7. a

Note to Teachers: The letters *a, g, t, q,* and *u* can look different in other fonts. Students should be able to recognize these letters in both versions.

Intro to Reading

4. Stories

3. Sentences

2. Words

1. Letters

Letters make up words.
Words make up sentences.
Sentences make up stories.

Intro to Reading

1. **Letters**

2. **Words**

pen	crown	mug
book	cake
hat	school	bed

3. **Sentence** — I like to read and write.

4. **Story**

   My First Day of School
   The school bell rings.
   Ring! Ring!
   I meet my teacher.
   My teacher smiles.
   It will be a great year!

Intro to Reading

1. Count the number of letters in each word. Letters include consonants and vowels.
2. Circle the vowel in each word.

1 nap	2 can	3 up	4 run
5 best	6 in	7 hop	8 sock
9 the	10 will	11 at	12 bus

Remember: Every word must have at least one vowel.

Intro to Reading

1. Listen to the story.
2. Count the number of words in each sentence.
3. Count the number of sentences in the story.

I Wish I Could Read!

The house is so quiet.

Where is everyone?

Dad is reading the mail.

Mom is reading her recipe book.

Sister is reading her library book.

Brother is reading his newsletter.

I wish I could read, too!

I just cannot wait to learn to read.

Kid in the Middle

Kid in the Middle:

Kid in the Middle refers to a **CVC** (consonant-vowel-consonant) word. The vowel has a short sound.

- - - - - - - -

Tell students: "Three kids enjoy walking alongside each other. The **shortest** kid always walks in the middle. Since he is so young, he does not even know how to say his own name, which is *a, e, i, o,* or *u*. When people ask him his name, he just answers with a **short** vowel sound: /ă/, /ĕ/, /ĭ/, /ŏ/, or /ŭ/. He also doesn't know how to wear a hat properly. He wears it upside down." Draw stick figures like the ones shown below to demonstrate the story. Write CVC words into the heads using different vowels. Show the marking of the short vowel sound, which looks like an upside down hat.

Kid in the Middle

1. ran   mad   man

2. pad   nap   ram

3. sad   tan   mat

rat

The hint for the sound of ă is *apple*.

Kid in the Middle

1. can   fat   cap

2. gap   rag   bad

3. tab   fan   tag

4. bat   bag   had

Kid in the Middle

MARK THE WORD

ă

1. Draw a ˘ above the *Kid in the Middle* vowel.
2. Say the vowel sound.
3. Read the word.

1.  săt   măp   păt   tăd

2. căt   săg   băn   căb

nonsense words

3. năd   săn   năm   dăt

4. făp   măb   găn   făm

WRITE

a

The

The man

The man ran

The man ran on

The man ran on the

The man ran on the mat.

a

The

The fat

The fat cat

The fat cat sat

The fat cat sat on

The fat cat sat on the

The fat cat sat on the bat.

Color all the pictures that have the ă sound.

1. Write an a in the shaded box.
2. Read the word.
3. Draw a picture of the word in the box.

1 b a g	2 h a t	3 m a p
4 c a p	5 m a n	6 f a n
7 p a d	8 c a n	9 p a n

1. Say the name of the picture.
2. Circle the words that rhyme with the picture.

1	🧢	(gap)	bad	(tap)
2	🏏	nag	(fat)	(sat)
3	🌀	(tan)	mad	(ran)

1. Say the name of the picture.
2. Draw a line from the picture to the word that rhymes with it.

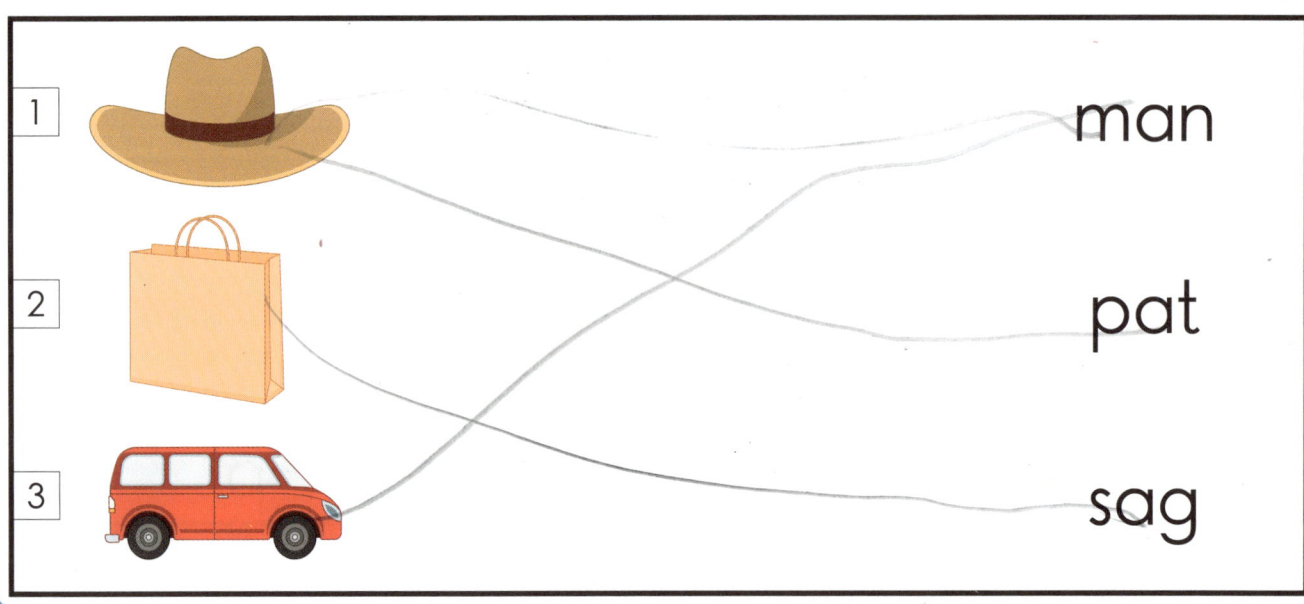

ACTIVITY

a

Fill the circles with letters to make the ă *Kid in the Middle* words shown in the pictures. Use letters from the boxes below.

t a g

first letter choices

b
c
f
h
p
t̶

last letter choices

g̶
g
n
n
t
t

29

Phonics Skill: a

Pop Words: a the is on

POP WORDS

a

1. A cat ran.
2. A man ran.
3. A dad ran.
4. A rat ran.

the

5. The dad had a nap.
6. The cat had a nap.
7. The rat had a nap.
8. The man had a nap.

is

9. Is the cat fat?
10. The cat is fat.
11. Is the man sad?
12. The man is sad.

on

13. The 👟 is on the mat.
14. The 👔 is on the man.
15. The 🐞 is on the bat.
16. The 🎀 is on the bag.

Pop Words: | a | the | is | on |

1. a   is   on   the

2. Is   The   A   On

3. the   on   a   is

4. on   A   The   Is

Phonics Skill: a

Pop Words: a · the · is · on

POP WORDS

1. Read the sentence.
2. Circle the picture that matches the sentence.

1 A tag is on the bag.		
2 The cat is on a mat.		
3 The man is sad.		
4 A pad is on the cap.		
5 The hat is on the dad.		

32

Kid in the Middle

1. hid   sit   dip

2. pit   hit   bib

3. fit   rid   dim

rip

The hint for the sound of ĭ is *itch*.

Note to Teachers:

Kid in the Middle

1. kid   dig   bit

2. tip   bid   him

3. nit   sip   fin

4. did   lit   rib

Kid in the Middle

MARK THE WORD

ĭ

1. Draw a ˘ above the *Kid in the Middle* vowel.
2. Say the vowel sound.
3. Read the word.

1.  hĭp   rĭm   tĭn   lĭd

2. kĭt   bĭn   lĭp   fĭg

nonsense words

3. hĭg   fĭm   dĭt   mĭg

4. lĭn   bĭp   tĭb   nĭd

WRITE

i

The

The big

The big pin

The big pin is

The big pin is on

The big pin is on the

The big pin is on the bib.

i

The

The kid

The kid did

The kid did sit

The kid did sit and

The kid did sit and dig.

ACTIVITY

Color all the pictures that have the ĭ sound.

38

ACTIVITY

i

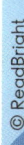

1. Write an **i** in the shaded box.
2. Read the word.
3. Draw a picture of the word in the box.

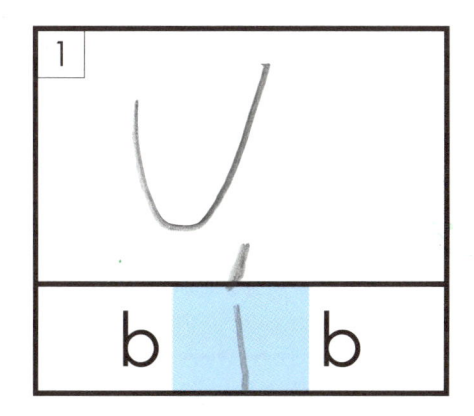

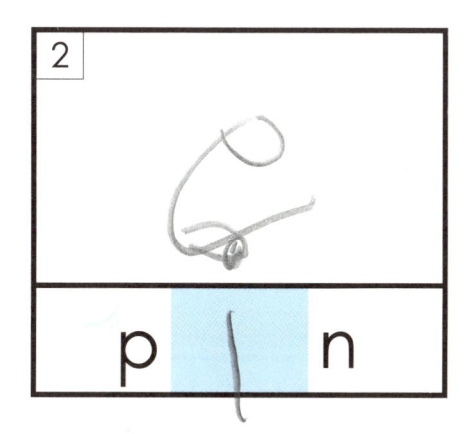

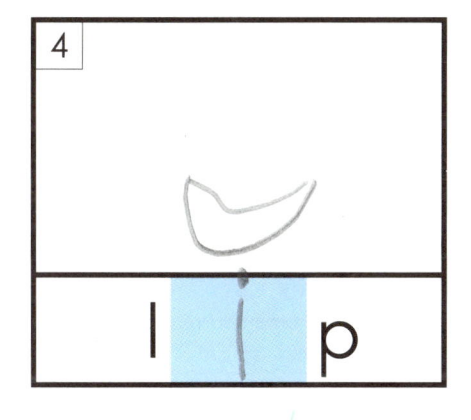

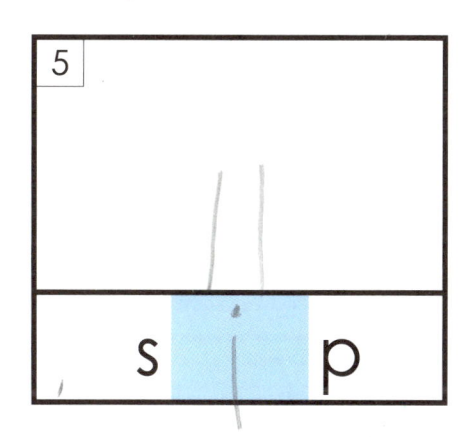

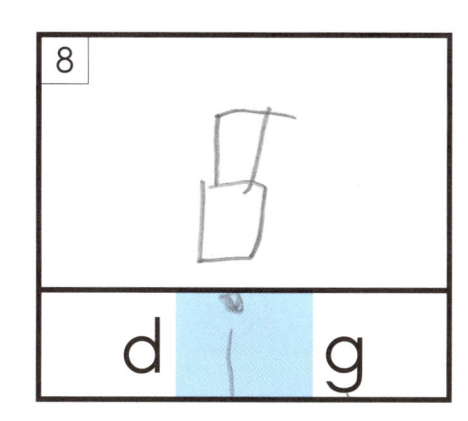

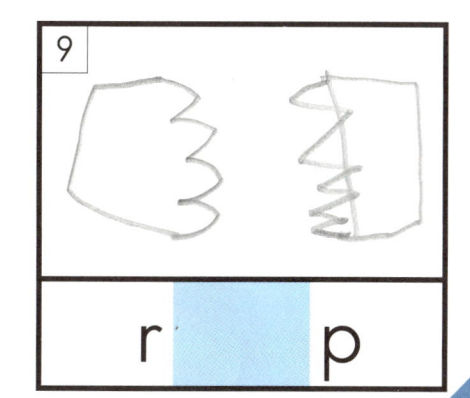

1 b _ b	2 p _ n	3 k _ d
4 l _ p	5 s _ p	6 p _ t
7 s _ t	8 d _ g	9 r _ p

39

ACTIVITY

i

1. Say the name of the picture.
2. Circle the words that *rhyme* with the picture.

1	(bib)	rib	dig	fib
2	(kid)	fin	hid	lid
3	(rip)	hip	rim	dip

1. Say the name of the picture.
2. Draw a line from the picture to the word that *rhymes* with it.

1	(lips)		bin
2	(pin)		fig
3	(wig)		sip

40

ACTIVITY
i

Fill the circles with letters to make the ĭ *Kid in the Middle* words shown in the pictures. Use letters from the boxes below.

first letter choices

~~b~~
~~d~~
k
l
p
w

last letter choices

b
d
g
n
p

Kid in the Middle

1. lid   nag   win

2. big   pal   nip

3. lap   sin   rim

4. hat   lag   wig

ACTIVITY

a•i

1. Look at the picture.
2. Circle the word that matches the picture.

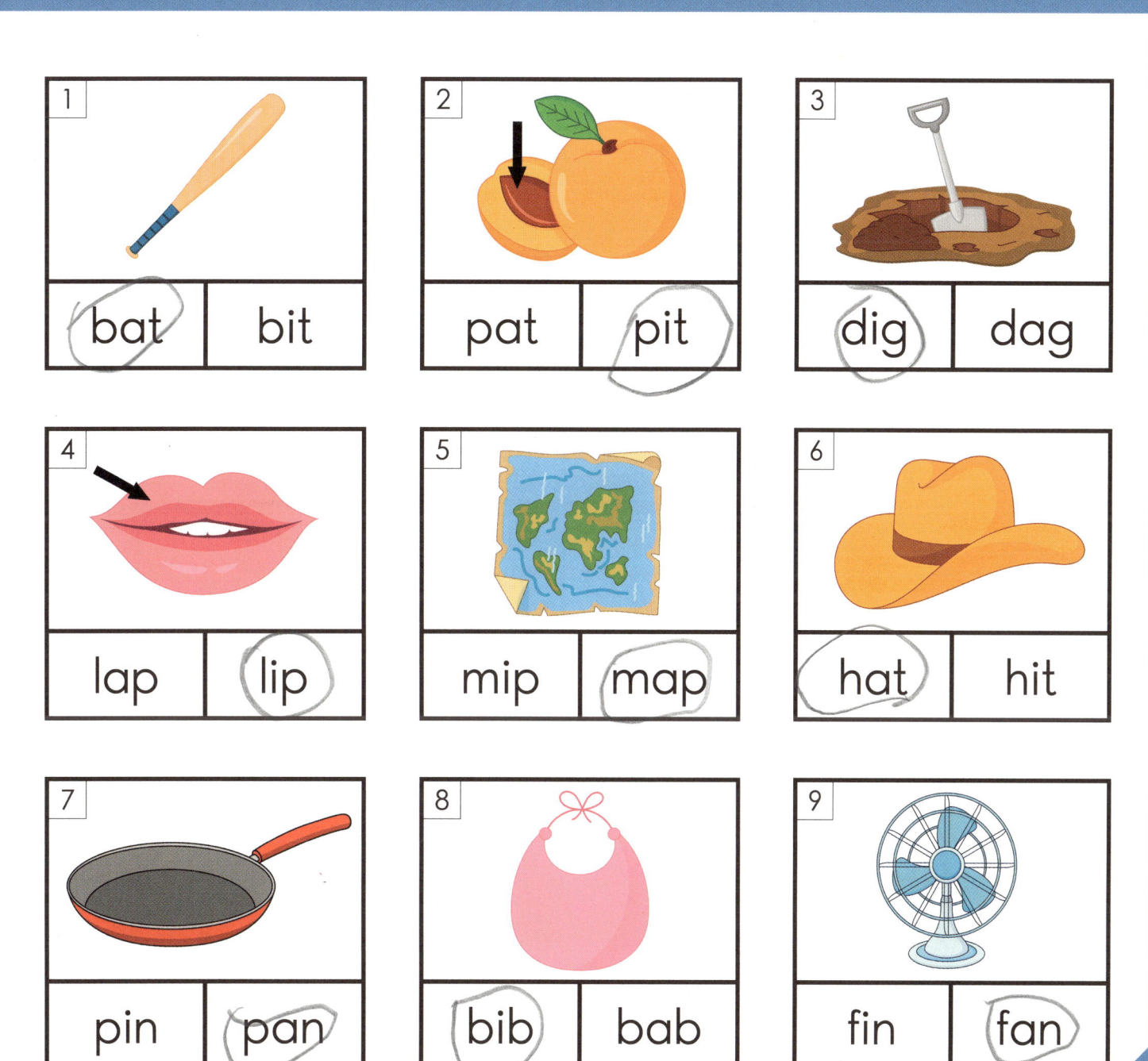

1	2	3
(bat) / bit	pat / (pit)	(dig) / dag

4	5	6
lap / (lip)	mip / (map)	(hat) / hit

7	8	9
pin / (pan)	(bib) / bab	fin / (fan)

ACTIVITY

a·i

1. Say the name of the picture.
2. Look at the pairs of letters beside each picture.
3. Shade in the letter in each pair that is in the word.
4. Write the word in the empty boxes at the end of the row.

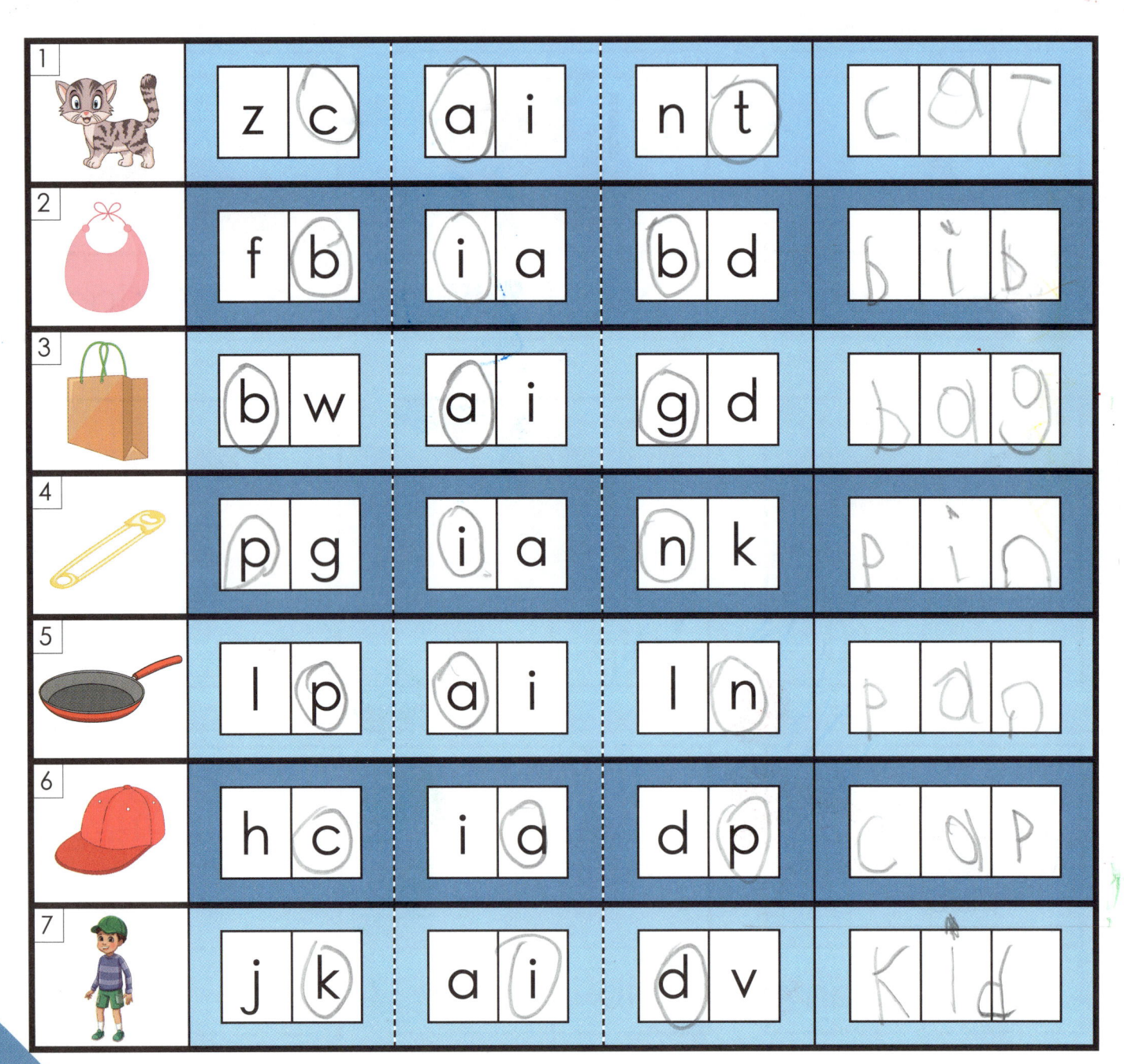

#					
1	🐱	z **c**	**a** i	**n** t	c a t
2	👶 bib	f **b**	**i** a	**b** d	b i b
3	🛍️	**b** w	**a** i	**g** d	b a g
4	🧷	**p** g	**i** a	**n** k	p i n
5	🍳	l **p**	**a** i	l **n**	p a n
6	🧢	h **c**	**i** d	d **p**	c i p
7	🧒	j **k**	**a** i	**d** v	k i d

review

44

Phonics Skill: i

Pop Words: I have of and

POP WORDS

I

1. I can dig.
2. I can nap.
3. I can sit.
4. I can tap.

have

5. I have a bib.
6. I have a hat.
7. I have a wig.
8. I have a bat.

of

9. I have a bit of .
10. I have a bit of .
11. I have a bit of .
12. I have a bit of .

and

13. I sit and dig.
14. I sit and tap.
15. I sit and sip.
16. I sit and nap.

45

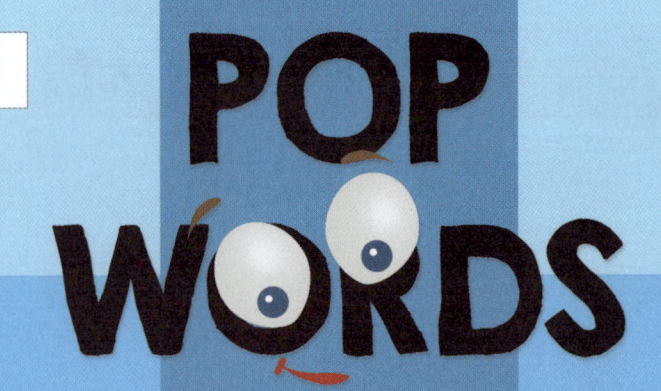

Pop Words: | I | have | of | and |

POP WORDS

1. I have of and

2. the is on a

3. and A have on

4. of is The I

Phonics Skill: i

Pop Words: I have of and

POP WORDS

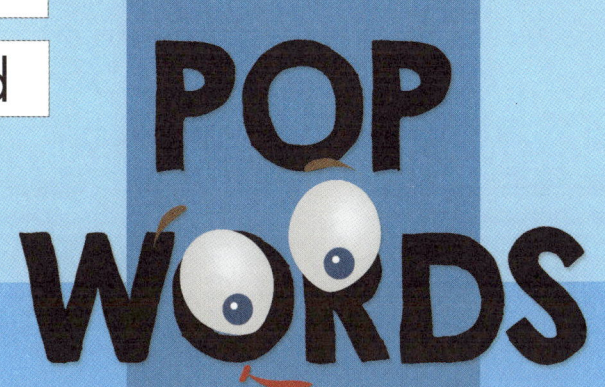

1. Read the sentence.
2. Circle the picture that matches the sentence.

1	The man and the kid have a hat.		
2	I ran and ran.		
3	The bib and the rag have a rip.		
4	I can sit and sip.		
5	Can I have a bit of it?		

47

Kid in the Middle

1. top   rot   pot

2. hop   lot   cot

3. mop   fox   hot

4. not

Note to Teachers: The hint for the sound of ŏ is *octopus*.

Kid in the Middle

1. cob   nod   jog

2. rod   job   fog

3. rob   pod   sob

                                              log

The /ŏ/ sometimes has a slightly different sound.

Kid in the Middle

ŏ

MARK THE WORD

1. Draw a ˘ above the *Kid in the Middle* vowel.
2. Say the vowel sound.
3. Read the word.

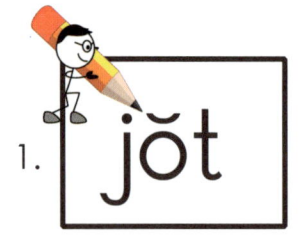

1. jŏt   dŏt   pŏp   gŏt

2. hŏg   Mŏm   mŏb   nŏd

---

nonsense words

3. bŏt   jŏp   mŏt   rŏp

4. pŏb   vŏg   dŏd   fŏt

WRITE

o

The

The hot

The hot pot

The hot pot is

The hot pot is not

The hot pot is not big.

o

The

The fox

The fox is

The fox is on

The fox is on top

The fox is on top of

The fox is on top of the

The fox is on top of the box.

o

The

The dog

The dog can

The dog can jog

The dog can jog **on**

The dog can jog **on the**

The dog can jog **on the** log.

ACTIVITY 0

Color all the pictures that have the ŏ sound.

ACTIVITY

o

1. Write an o in the shaded box.
2. Read the word.
3. Draw a picture of the word in the box.

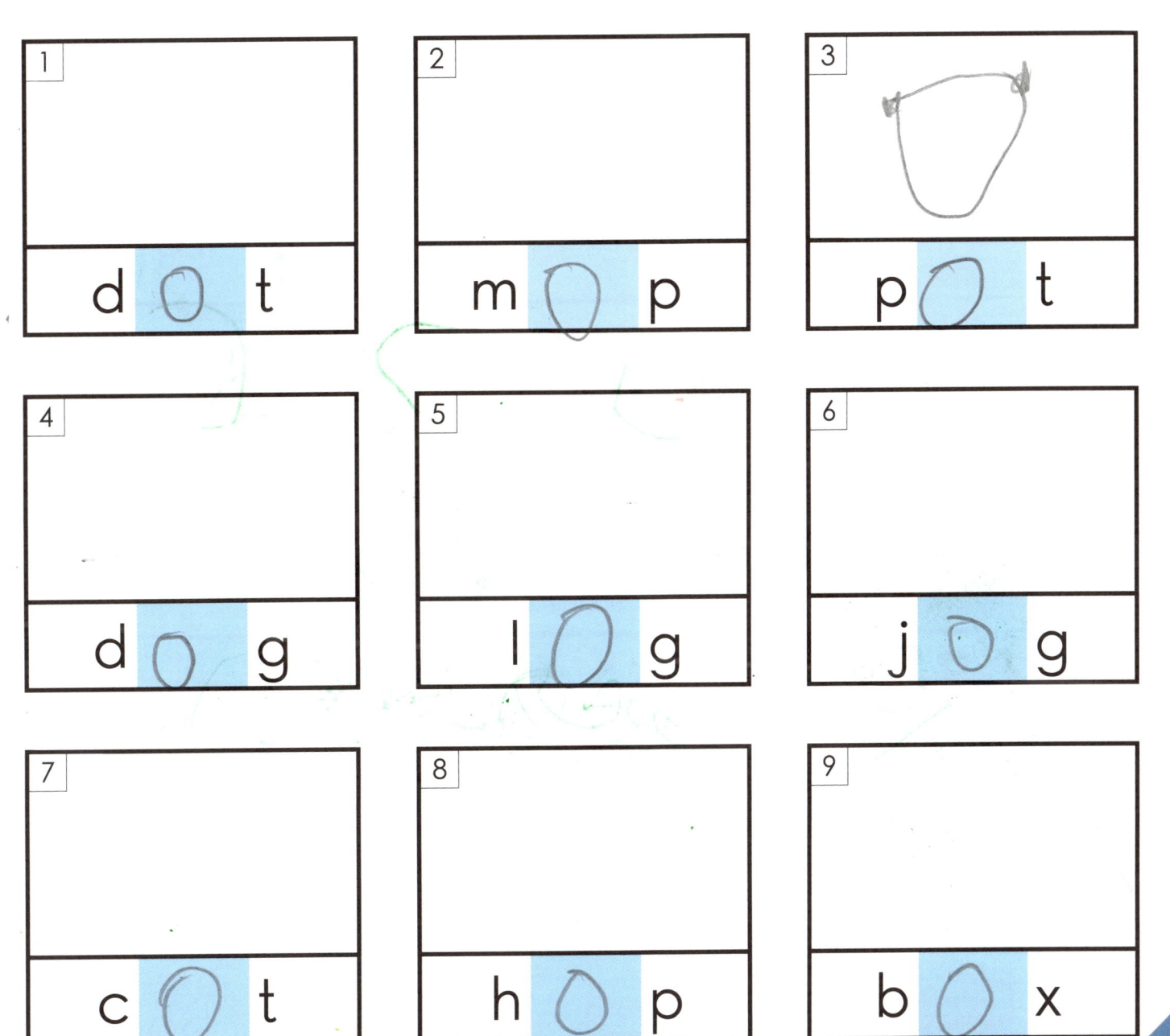

1	2	3
d o t	m o p	p o t

4	5	6
d o g	l o g	j o g

7	8	9
c o t	h o p	b o x

ACTIVITY 0

1. Say the name of the picture.
2. Circle the words that rhyme with the picture.

1	●	hot	dog	(not)
2	🧹	cop	top	rot
3	👶	log	(rob)	(job)

1. Say the name of the picture.
2. Draw a line from the picture to the word that rhymes with it.

fog

fox

pop

56

ACTIVITY

o

Fill the circles with letters to make the ŏ *Kid in the Middle* words shown in the pictures. Use letters from the boxes below.

first letter choices
b
f
l
m
p
p

last letter choices
g
p
p
t
x
x

57

Kid in the Middle

1. sop   hip   got

2. van   gag   six

3. jam   pin   dot

4. mix   cop   sag

ACTIVITY

a·i·o

1. Look at the picture.
2. Circle the word that matches the picture.

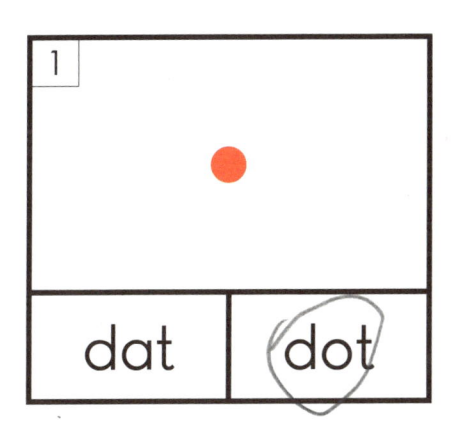

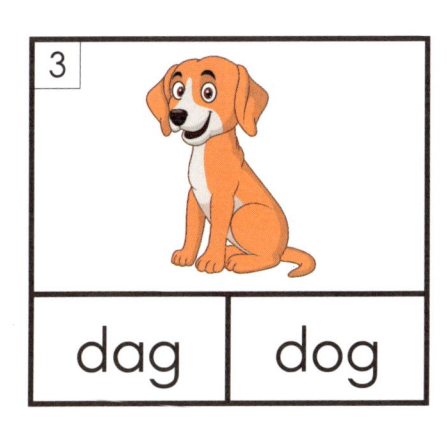

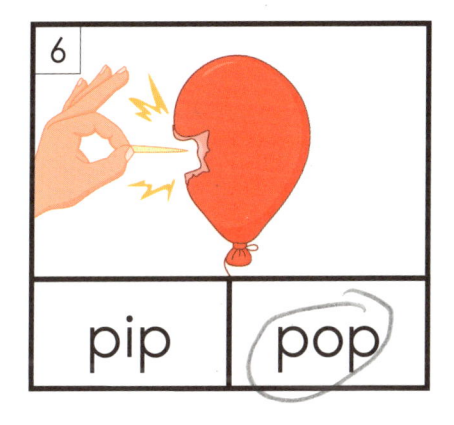

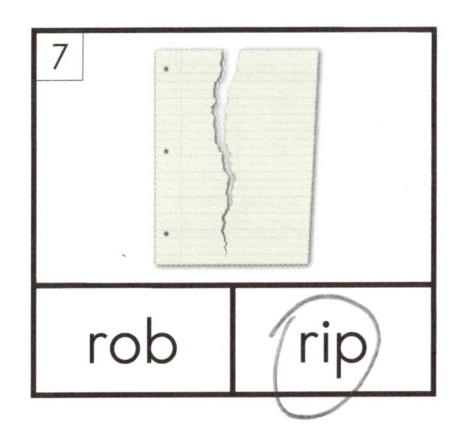

1	dat	(dot)
2	(sad)	sod
3	dag	(dog)
4	(pin)	pan
5	(nap)	nop
6	pip	(pop)
7	rob	(rip)
8	(lag)	(log)
9	(sob)	sib

ACTIVITY

a·i·o

1. Say the name of the picture.
2. Look at the pairs of letters beside each picture.
3. Shade in the letter in each pair that is in the word.
4. Write the word in the empty boxes at the end of the row.

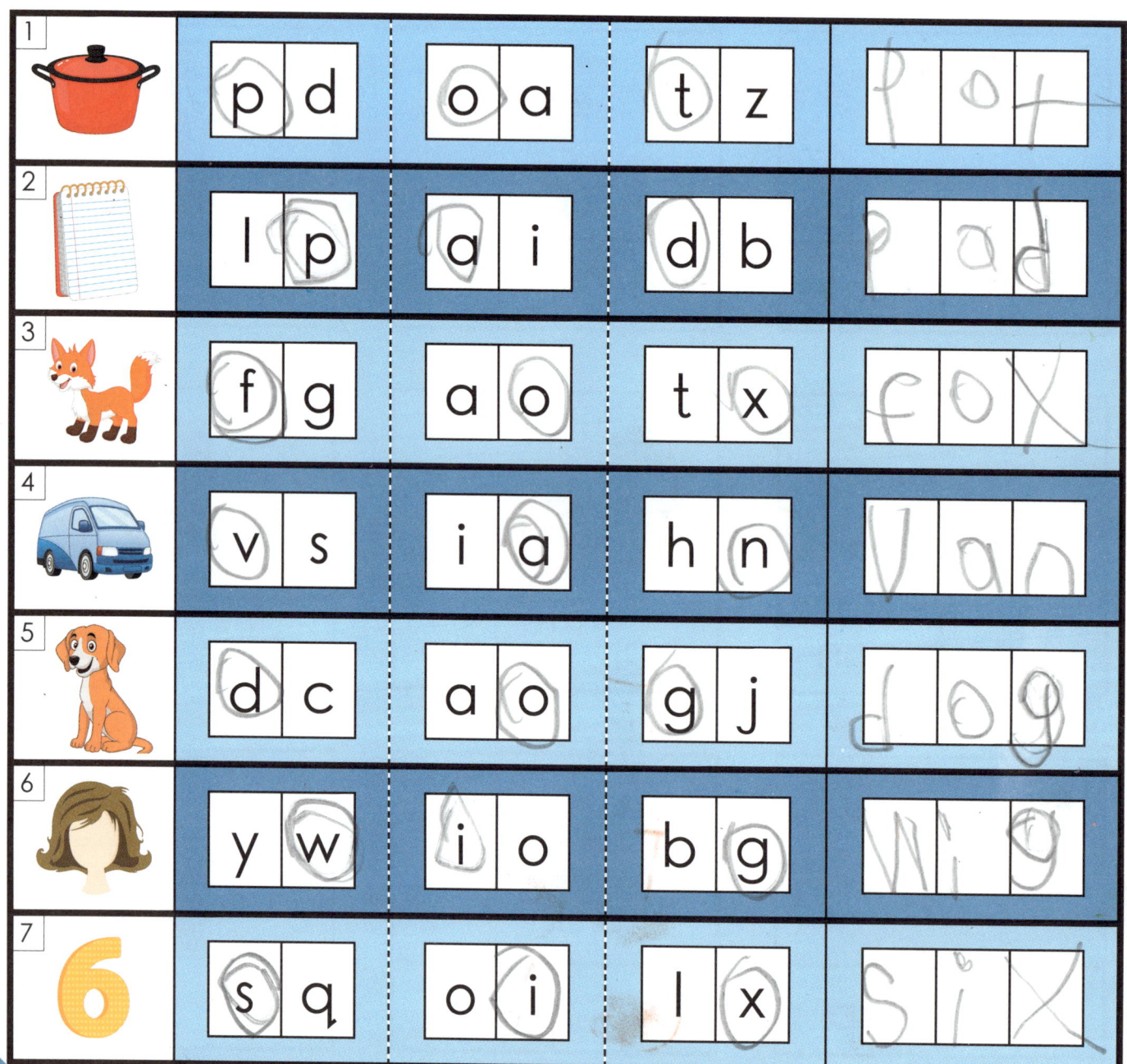

#					
1	pot	p d	o a	t z	pot
2	notepad	l p	a i	d b	pad
3	fox	f g	a o	t x	fox
4	van	v s	i a	h n	van
5	dog	d c	a o	g j	dog
6	wig	y w	i o	b g	wig
7	6	s q	o i	l x	six

Phonics Skill: o

Pop Words: has you

POP WORDS

has

1. The bag has a rip.
2. The bib has a rip.
3. The rag has a rip.
4. The cap has a rip.

you

5. Can you hop? You can hop.
6. Can you nap? You can nap.
7. Can you jog? You can jog.
8. Can you win? You can win.

has	you

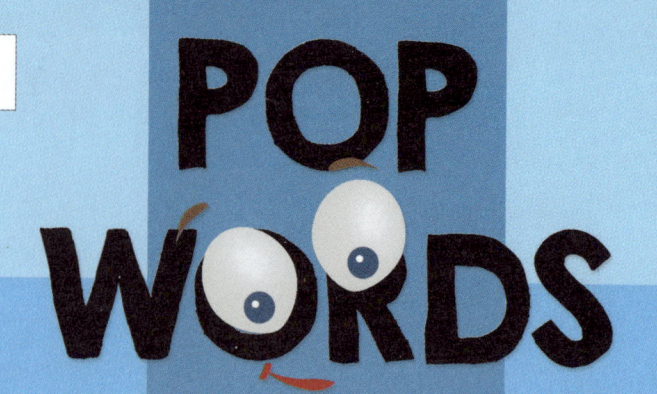

POP WORDS

1. has   you   and   I

2. of   have   has   You

3. the   a   you   is

4. on   and   have   has

Phonics Skill: o

Pop Words: has, you

POP WORDS

1. Read the sentence.
2. Circle the picture that matches the sentence.

1	You can hop.
2	You have a big cap.
3	The box has a big pot on it.
4	You can sit on the log.
5	The mop has a hat on it.

Kid in the Middle

1. cup   nut   run

2. bus   cub   jug

3. cut   mud   gum

4. hug

Note to Teachers: The hint for the sound of ŭ is *umbrella*.

Kid in the Middle

1. hut   bug   sun

2. rub   mug   rum

3. tug   sum   cud

4. bun   fun   tub

Kid in the Middle

ŭ

MARK THE WORD

1. Draw a ⌣ above the *Kid in the Middle* vowel.
2. Say the vowel sound.
3. Read the word.

1. cŭt   dŭg   gŭm   sŭn

2. rŭb   hŭm   mŭd   rŭg

nonsense words

3. rŭd   cŭg   nŭg   bŭp

4. lŭn   pŭm   tŭt   jŭb

WRITE

u

The

The bug

The bug is

The bug is on

The bug is on the

The bug is on the rug.

u

The

The cup

The cup is

The cup is on

The cup is on the

The cup is on the pup.

ACTIVITY
u

Color all the pictures that have the ŭ sound.

ACTIVITY

u

1. Write a u in the shaded box.
2. Read the word.
3. Draw a picture of the word in the box.

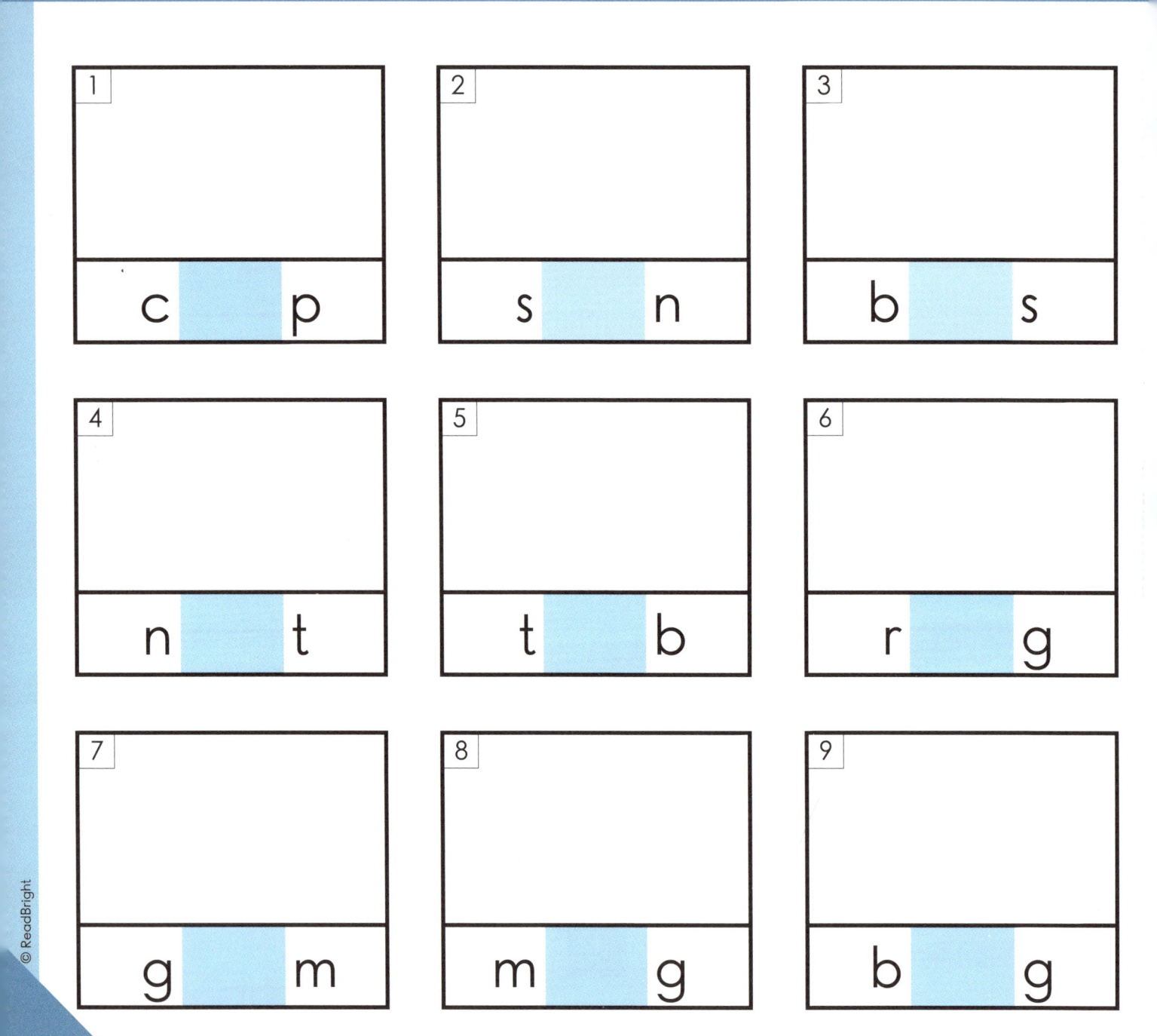

1 c p	2 s n	3 b s
4 n t	5 t b	6 r g
7 g m	8 m g	9 b g

70

ACTIVITY

u

1. Say the name of the picture.
2. Circle the words that rhyme with the picture.

1	☀️	bus	bun	fun
2	🐞	tug	rum	hug
3	✂️	cup	but	hut

1. Say the name of the picture.
2. Draw a line from the picture to the word that rhymes with it.

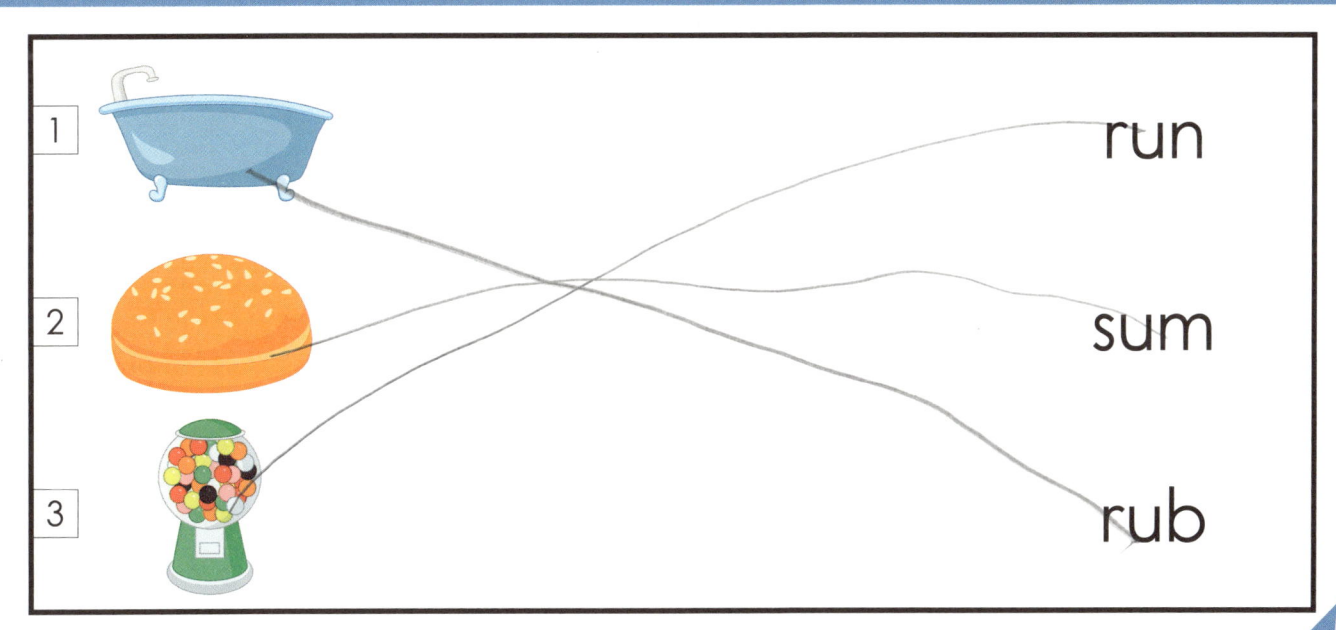

run

sum

rub

71

ACTIVITY

u

Fill the circles with letters to make the ŭ *Kid in the Middle* words shown in the pictures. Use letters from the boxes below.

first letter choices

b
b
b
c
g
s

last letter choices

g
m
n
n
p
s

72

Kid in the Middle

1. dug   tap   cot

2. box   hum   zip

3. lad   fix   rug

4. lip   pan   tot

ACTIVITY

a·i·o·u

1. Look at the picture.
2. Circle the word that matches the picture.

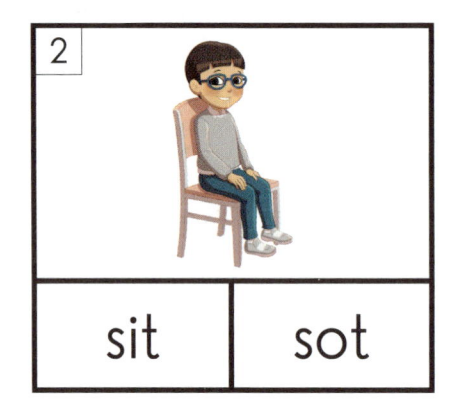

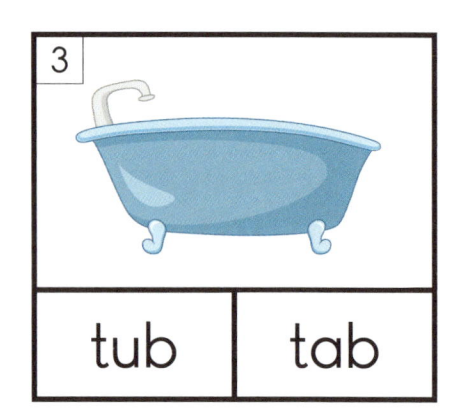

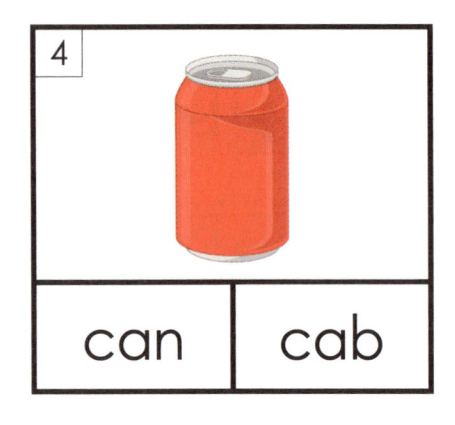

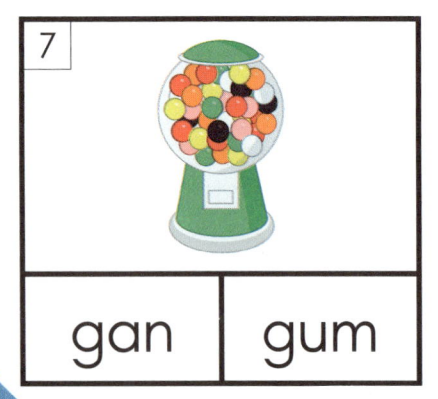

1	2	3
mop / mup	sit / sot	tub / tab

4	5	6
can / cab	mud / mug	hop / hom

7	8	9
gan / gum	pad / pod	hum / hut

74

ACTIVITY

a·i·o·u

1. Say the name of the picture.
2. Look at the pairs of letters beside each picture.
3. Shade in the letter in each pair that is in the word.
4. Write the word in the empty boxes at the end of the row.

1	hat	h n	a o	l t		
2	bun	f b	i u	n z		
3	bug	b n	u o	t g		
4	box	b d	o a	x j		
5	pit	p l	i o	t k		
6	cup	c g	o u	p d		
7	fan	l f	a i	n x		

75

Phonics Skill: u

Pop Words: to do his down

POP WORDS

to

1. I run to the 🚲. 
2. I run to the ✈️. 
3. I run to the 🪑. 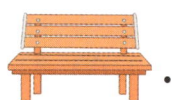
4. I run to the 🏐.

do

5. I do not hop on a cot.
6. I do not hop on a bus.
7. I do not hop on a pin.
8. I do not hop on a rag.

his

9. The man has his kit.
10. The man has his cup.
11. The man has his hat.
12. The man has his mop.

down

13. I sat down on the rug.
14. I sat down on the can.
15. I sat down on the box.
16. I sat down on the log.

76

Pop Words: | to | do | his | down

POP WORDS

1. his   to   do   down

2. I   has   his   is

3. do   to   you   of

4. and   down   have   the

Phonics Skill: u

Pop Words: to do his down

POP WORDS

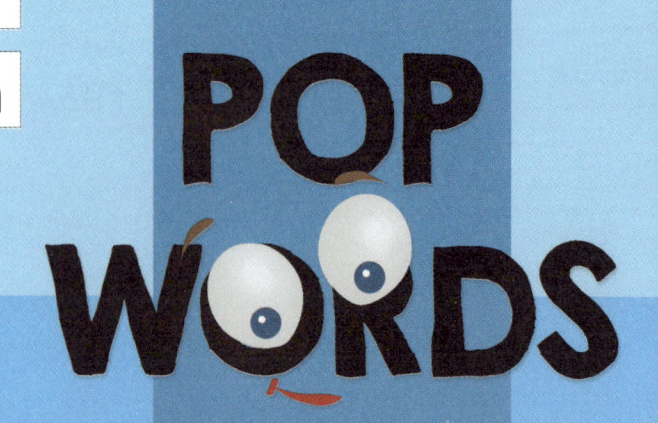

1. Read the sentence.
2. Circle the picture that matches the sentence.

1	The bug ran down the bat.		
2	The kid sat down on his mat.		
3	You can run to the tub.		
4	The man ran to his bus.		
5	I do not mop.		

78

Kid in the Middle

1. bet   set   bed

2. let   red   men

3. get   leg   ten

peg

The hint for the sound of ĕ is *elephant*.

Kid in the Middle

1. web   led   beg

2. pet   hen   wet

3. yes   net   hem

4. met   fed   den

READ

Kid in the Middle

ĕ

MARK THE WORD

1. Draw a ⌣ above the *Kid in the Middle* vowel.
2. Say the vowel sound.
3. Read the word.

1. bĕg • lĕg • gĕt • wĕd

2. fĕd • pĕn • mĕn • jĕt

nonsense words

3. kĕm • sĕn • yĕd • jĕg

4. vĕn • tĕb • fĕt • hĕp

WRITE

81

e

The

The red

The red hen

The red hen sat

The red hen sat on

The red hen sat on the

The red hen sat on the bed.

e

Ten

Ten men

Ten men met

Ten men met **on**

Ten men met **on a**

Ten men met **on a** bus.

ACTIVITY
e

Color all the pictures that have the ĕ sound.

ACTIVITY

e

1. Write an e in the shaded box.
2. Read the word.
3. Draw a picture of the word in the box.

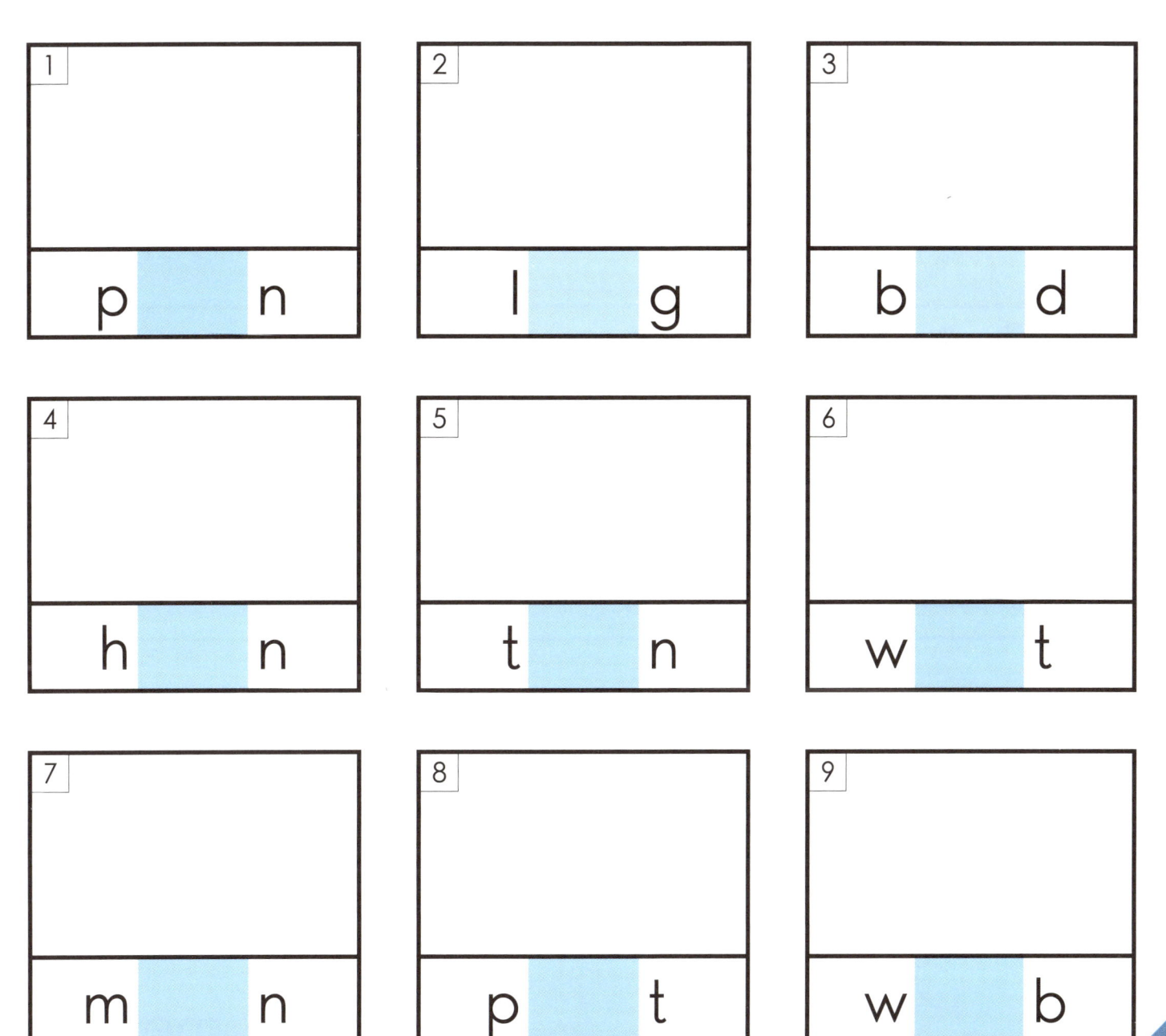

1 p n	2 l g	3 b d
4 h n	5 t n	6 w t
7 m n	8 p t	9 w b

85

ACTIVITY e

1. Say the name of the picture.
2. Circle the words that rhyme with the picture.

1		get	hem	let
2		peg	hen	den
3		pen	ten	fed

1. Say the name of the picture.
2. Draw a line from the picture to the word that rhymes with it.

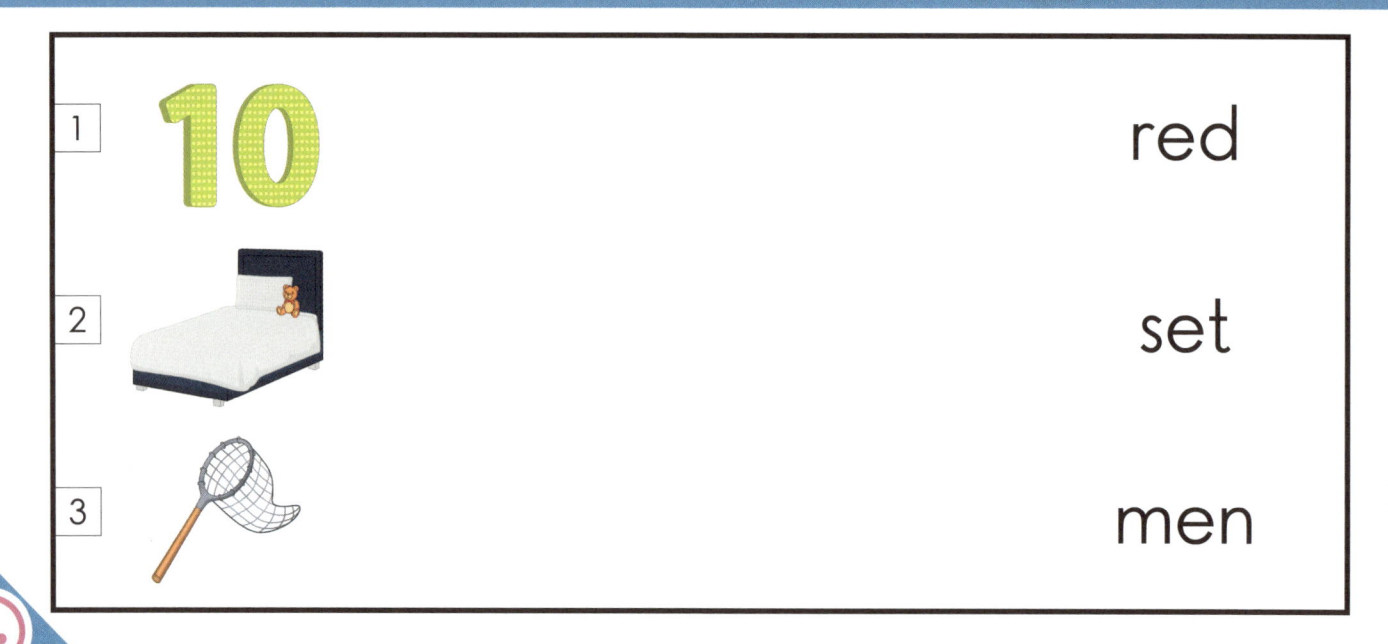

1. 10 — red
2. (bed) — set
3. (net) — men

ACTIVITY
e

Fill the circles with letters to make the ĕ *Kid in the Middle* words shown in the pictures. Use letters from the boxes below.

first letter choices

b
h
n
p
t
w

last letter choices

b
d
n
n
t

87

Kid in the Middle

	ă	ĕ	ă	ĕ
1.	tan	ten	pan	pen
2.	bat	bet	sat	set
3.	man	men	bad	bed
4.	pat	pet	lag	leg

Note to Teachers:

Extra practice pages are provided for *a* and *e*, as these sounds are easily confused because they sound alike.

Teach these words by reading across the grid (*tan, ten; pan, pen*). This will emphasize the contrast between the /ă/ and /ĕ/ sounds.

ACTIVITY

a·e

1. Look at the picture.
2. Write a or e in the box to complete the word.

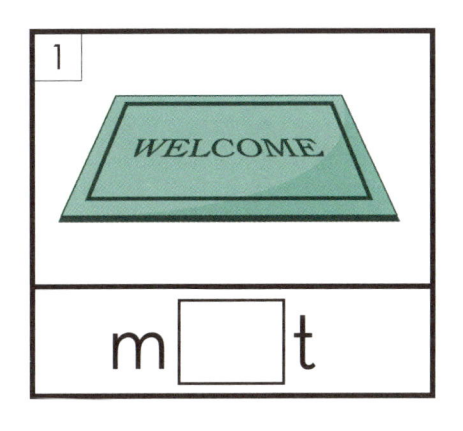

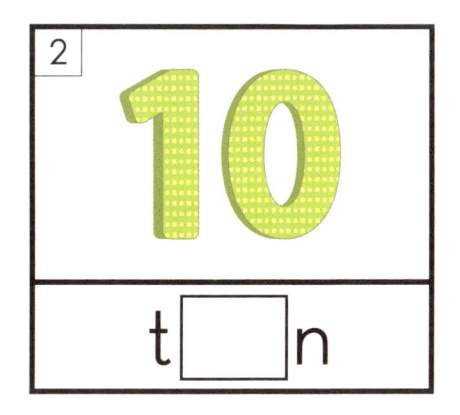

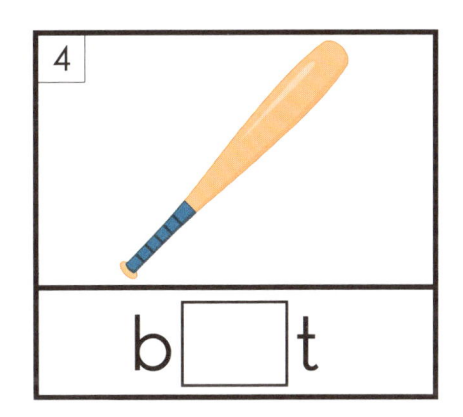

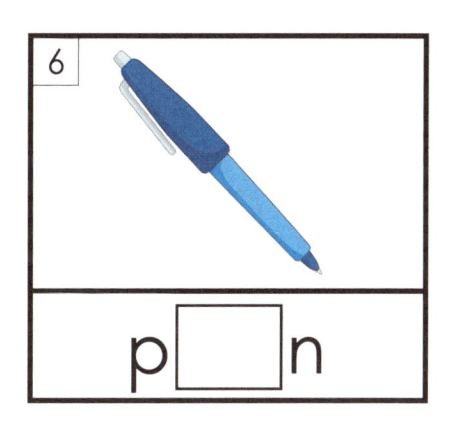

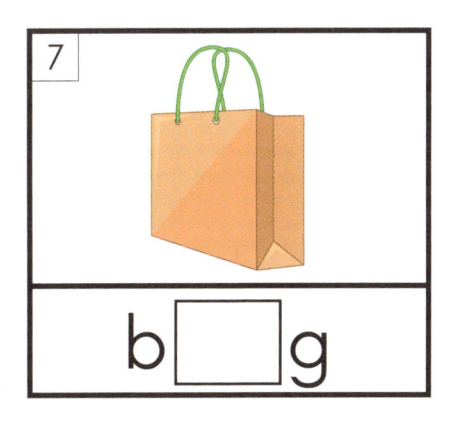

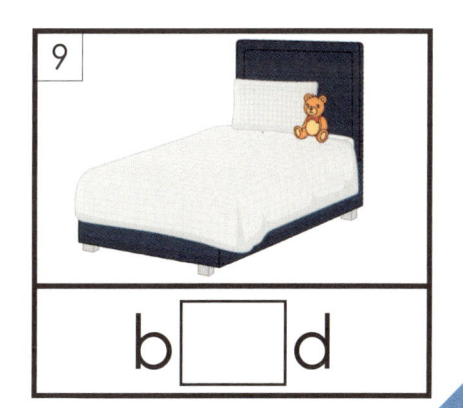

1	2	3
m☐t	t☐n	m☐n

4	5	6
b☐t	p☐t	p☐n

7	8	9
b☐g	p☐n	b☐d

Kid in the Middle

1. pun   yet   hop

2. tin   sat   met

3. jet   but   pod

4. zap   pot   bin

Kid in the Middle

ă
ĭ ŏ ŭ
ĕ

MARK THE WORD

1. Draw a ⌣ above the *Kid in the Middle* vowel.
2. Say the vowel sound.
3. Read the word.

1. cŭp   ram   pep   sip

2. hot   lit   jog   mug

nonsense words

3. han   vub   jit   mog

4. bem   lat   zob   ped

91

ACTIVITY

1. Look at the picture.
2. Circle the word that matches the picture.

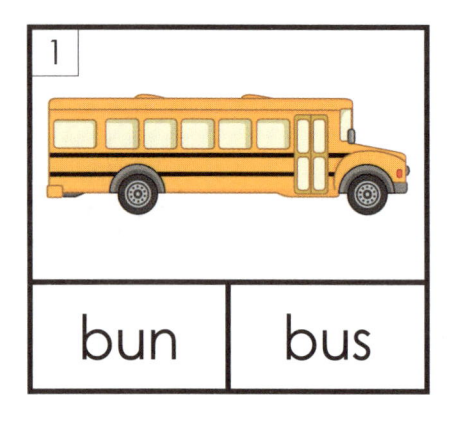

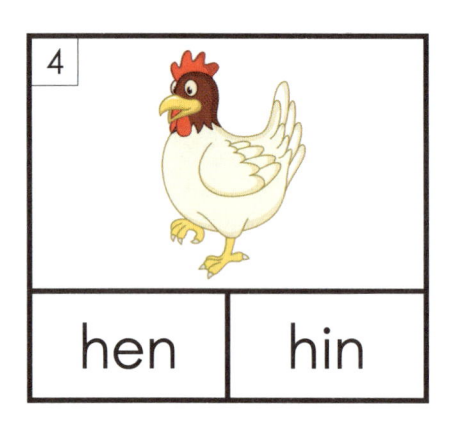

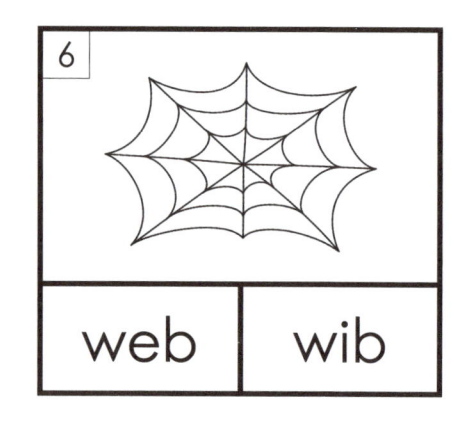

1	2	3
bun / bus	min / men	weg / wig

4	5	6
hen / hin	cat / cut	web / wib

7	8	9
mat / mut	pet / pit	fax / fox

1. Say the name of the picture.
2. Look at the pairs of letters beside each picture.
3. Shade in the letter in each pair that is in the word.
4. Write the word in the empty boxes at the end of the row.

1 	d b	e a	p d	
2 	n h	i e	t b	
3 	l z	e i	p g	
4 	t h	a o	g q	
5 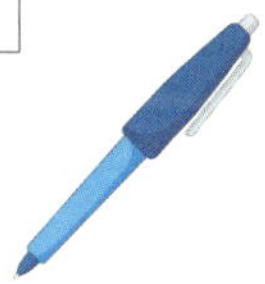	r p	e a	p n	
6 	s f	i u	n p	
7 	w c	e u	b s	

review

ACTIVITY

1. Read the sentences.
2. Circle all the *Kid in the Middle* words.
   (*Kid in the Middle* words have a vowel between two consonants.)
3. Write the circled words under the correct sunglasses below.

Fun in the Sun

1. I am a big kid.

2. I hop and jog.

3. I am hot and red.

4. I run to get a cap, a fan, and a mug.

5. I sit and nap on a mat.

6. Yes, it is fun in the sun!

ACTIVITY

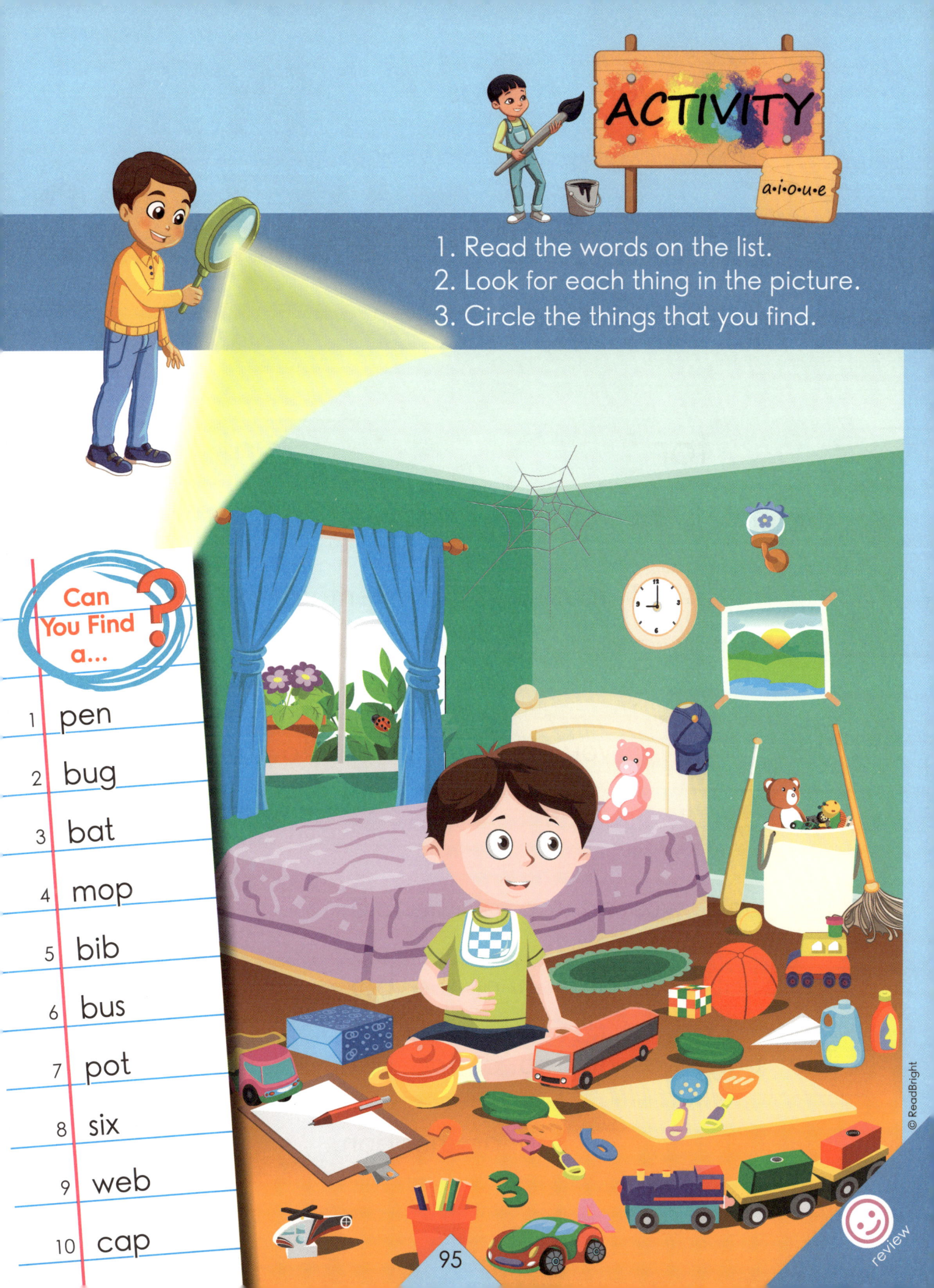

a·i·o·u·e

1. Read the words on the list.
2. Look for each thing in the picture.
3. Circle the things that you find.

Can You Find a...

1. pen
2. bug
3. bat
4. mop
5. bib
6. bus
7. pot
8. six
9. web
10. cap

95

Phonics Skill: e

Pop Words: for   went   was

POP WORDS

for

1. The net is for you.
2. The bun is for you.
3. The pot is for you.
4. The pin is for you.

went

5. I went to the 🛝. 
6. I went to the 🚂. 
7. I went to the 🚗. 
8. I went to the 🏠.

was

9. The pen was on top of the bib.
10. The hat was on top of the box.
11. The bug was on top of the bed.
12. The mug was on top of the pan.

Pop Words: for | went | was

POP WORDS

1. for   was   went   and

2. down   to   do   for

3. you   went   has   his

4. was   have   of   the

Phonics Skill: e

Pop Words: for | went | was

POP WORDS

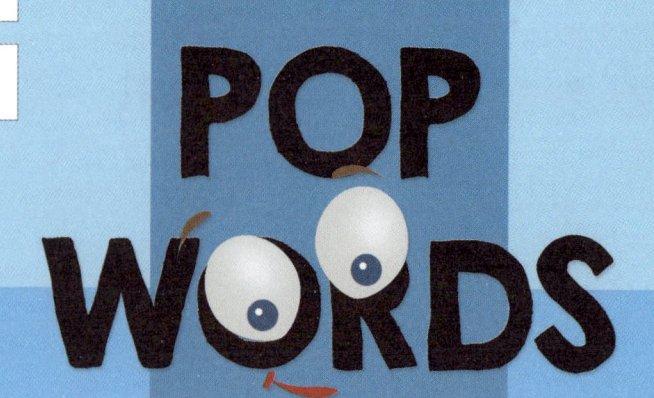

1. Read the sentence.
2. Circle the picture that matches the sentence.

1 The men went to the bus.		
2 The big box is for you.		
3 The hen went to the bug.		
4 The pen was on the pad.		
5 The kid was on the bed.		

98

Special Rules

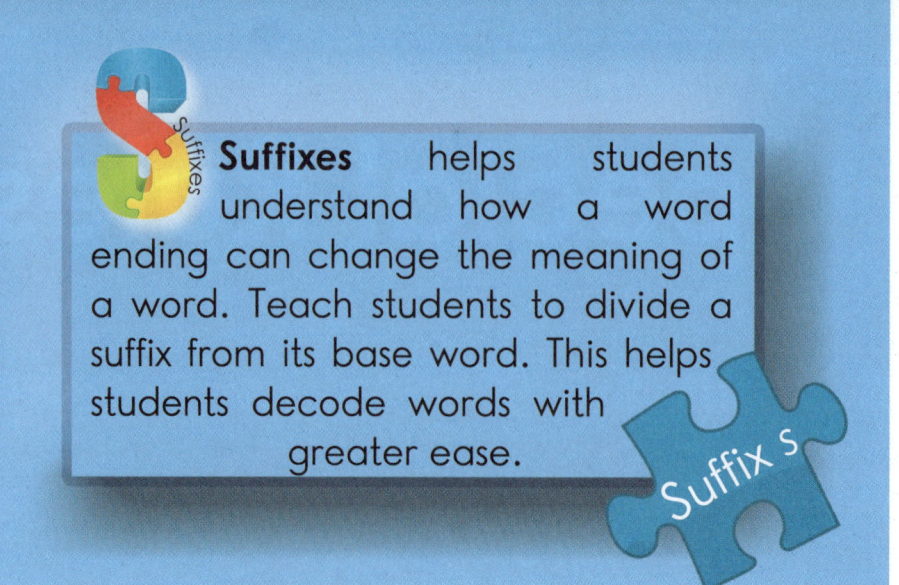

Special Rules

Suffixes helps students understand how a word ending can change the meaning of a word. Teach students to divide a suffix from its base word. This helps students decode words with greater ease.

Suffix s

Spelling Rules guides students to achieve proper spelling.

Double Letters
c or k

Special Sounds teaches students those sounds which do not conform to typical phonics rules.

s
all

s

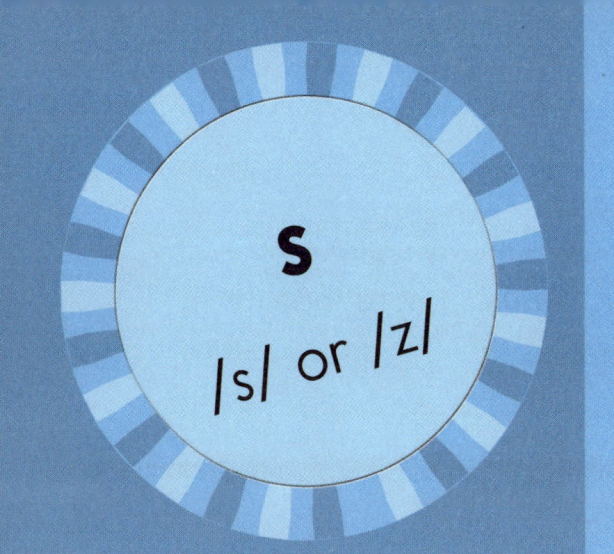

/s/ or /z/

The letter *s* always makes the /s/ sound at the beginning of a word. The letter *s* can make either the /s/ or /z/ sound in the middle of a word (*case/nose*) or at the end of a word (*bus/bags*).

/s/	1.	sat	sun
	2.	bus	yes
/z/	3.	as	is
	4.	has	his

READ

Suffix s

A suffix *s* can indicate a *plural* (more than one).

1.	cap		caps
2.	pin		pins
3.	dot		dots
4.	cup		cups
5.	pen		pens

Suffix s

A suffix *s* can indicate that a verb is in the present tense.

1.	nap	naps	sit	sits
2.	cut	cuts	hop	hops
3.	get	gets	pat	pats
4.	sip	sips	beg	begs
5.	pop	pops	run	runs

READ

Suffix s

Reminder: The letter s at the end of a word can have either the /s/ or /z/ sound.

To read words containing the suffix s:
- Cover the suffix s with your thumb.
- Read the base word.
- Lift your thumb.
- Read the whole word.

1. bats   mugs   cops
2. pets   taps   nuts
3. bins   cots   lets
4. figs   hugs   mats
5. sets   wins   jogs

Suffix s

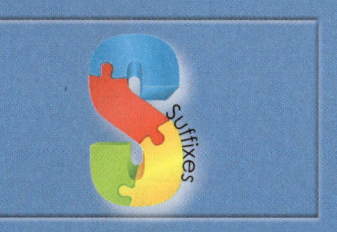

MARK THE WORD

1. Circle the suffix s.
2. Read the base word.
3. Read the whole word.

1. hit(s)   pad(s)   bug(s)   pot(s)

2. bed(s)   bun(s)   dip(s)   bag(s)

3. net(s)   mop(s)   hen(s)   tug(s)

4. tag(s)   hem(s)   sob(s)   rip(s)

Suffix s

The

The kid

The kid hops

The kid hops on

The kid hops on the

The kid hops on the pots,

The kid hops on the pots, pans,

The kid hops on the pots, pans, and

The kid hops on the pots, pans, and cups.

ACTIVITY

Suffix s

1. Look at the picture.
2. Circle the word that matches the picture.

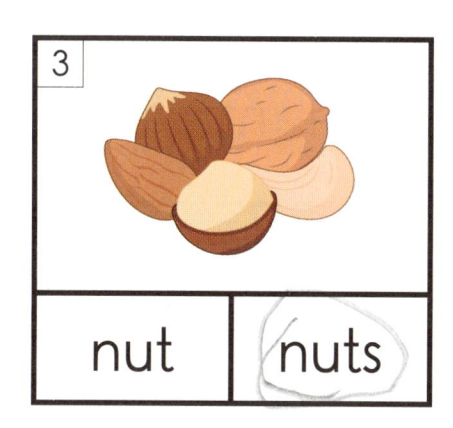

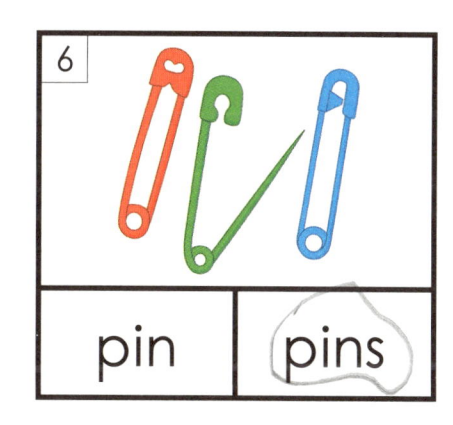

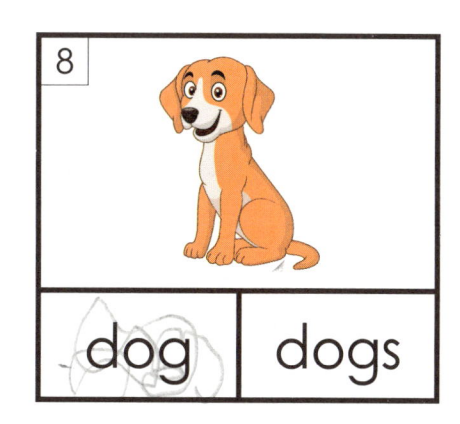

#	word 1	word 2
1	bat	**(bats)**
2	**(bib)**	bibs
3	nut	**(nuts)**
4	**(bed)**	beds
5	**(hen)**	hens
6	pin	**(pins)**
7	cup	**(cups)**
8	**(dog)**	dogs
9	bag	**(bags)**

107

ACTIVITY

Suffix s

1. Read the sentence.
2. Draw a picture of the sentence in the box.

1 The man digs.	
2 The hen sits.	
3 The kid sips.	
4 The man jogs.	
5 The bug runs.	
6 The cat naps.	
7 The kid hops.	

Phonics Skill: Suffix s

Pop Words: he me she be we

POP WORDS

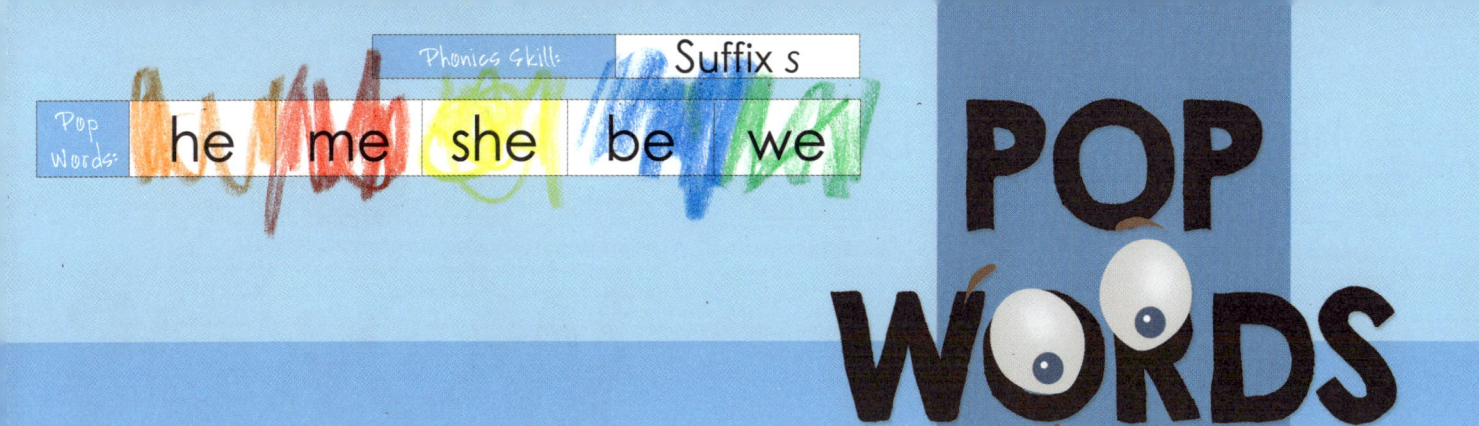

he | me

1. Can he run to me?
2. He can run to me.
3. Can he hop to me?
4. He can hop to me.

she

5. She hops on the mat.
6. She jogs on the mat.
7. She sits on the mat.
8. She naps on the mat.

be

9. I can be a 🤡 .
10. I can be a 👨‍🚒 .
11. I can be a 👮 .
12. I can be a 🤴 .

we

13. We can pet the cubs.
14. We can pet the hens.
15. We can pet the cats.
16. We can pet the dogs.

Pop Words: | he | me | she | be | we

POP WORDS

1. we   me   he   be

2. she   for   went   me

3. do   down   be   she

4. we   was   he   to

Phonics Skill: Suffix s

Pop Words: he | me | she | be | we

POP WORDS

1. Read the sentence.
2. Circle the picture that matches the sentence.

1	She sips and jogs.
2	The bug runs to me.
3	Do not be sad.
4	He sits on a box.
5	We have lots of bags.

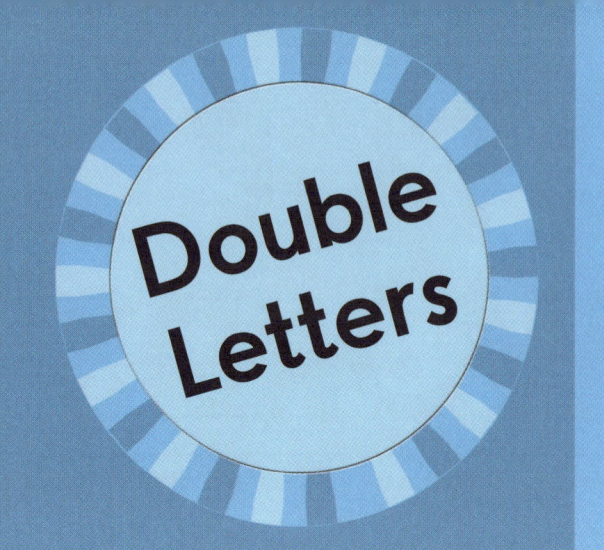

Double Letters

Spelling Rules: The letters *f*, *l*, *s*, and *z* are doubled when they appear at the end of a CVC word.

This sentence will help you remember the Double Letter Rule:

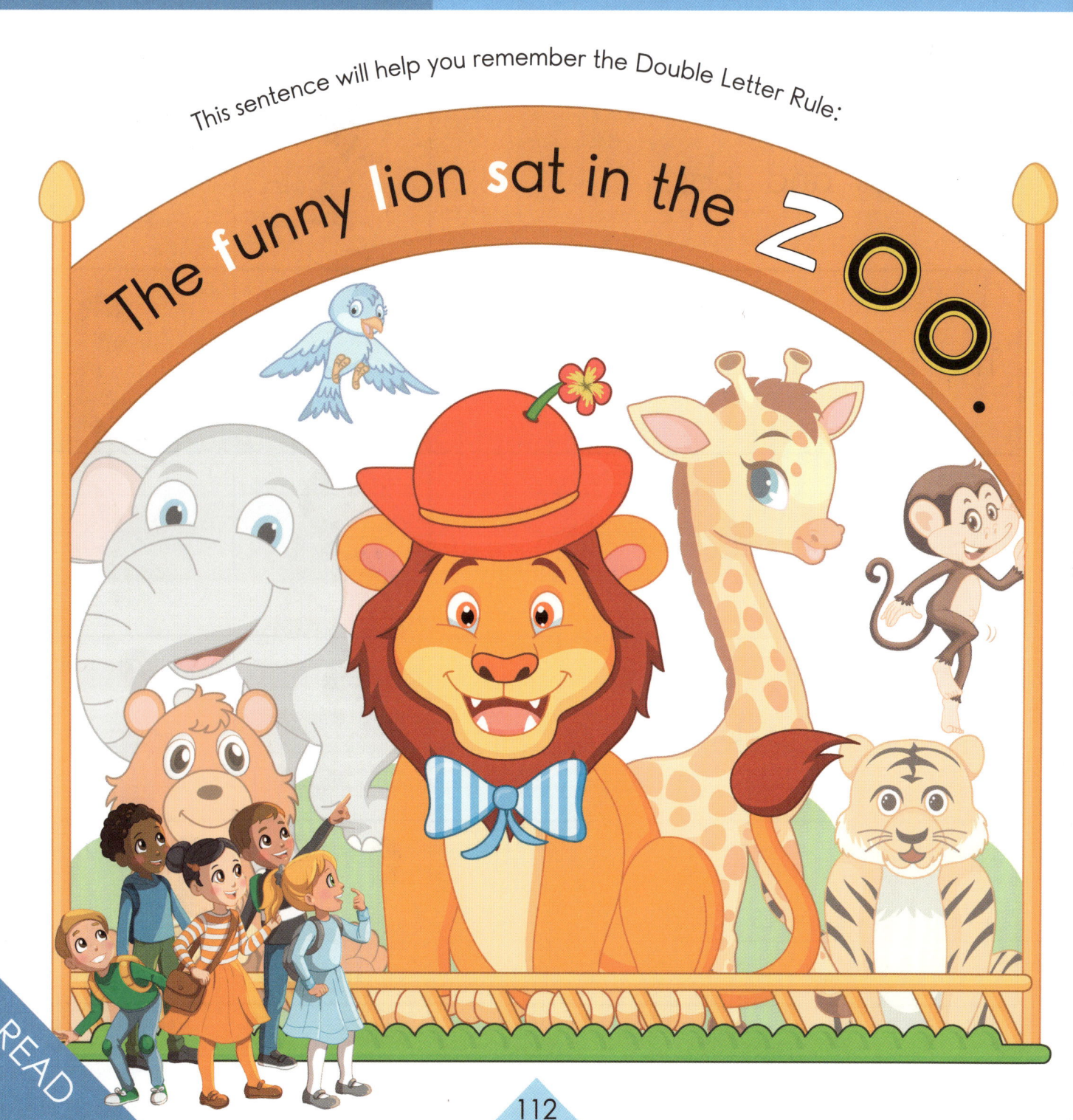

The funny lion sat in the zoo.

Double Letters

Read the double letters as one sound.

1.	**ff**	cuff	muff	huff
2.	**ll**	hill	fell	sell
3.	**ss**	less	pass	miss
4.	**zz**	buzz	fizz	fuzz

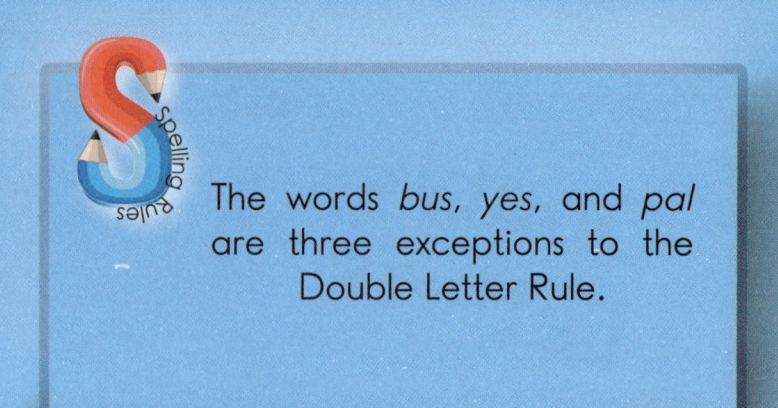

Double Letters

Spelling Rules: The words *bus*, *yes*, and *pal* are three exceptions to the Double Letter Rule.

1. fuss   buff   fill
2. yell   mass   buzz
3. puff   pill   tell
4. kiss   fuzz   mess

READ

Double Letters

MARK THE WORD

ll ff ss zz

1. Underline the double letters.
2. Say the sound of the double letters.
3. Read the word.

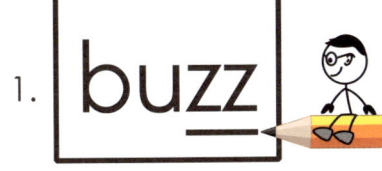

1. buzz   well   pass   huff

2. mess   cuff   fizz   bill

nonsense words

3. vill   pezz   baff   nuss

4. niff   tass   rozz   mell

ff

The

The man

The man did

The man did hu__ff__

The man did hu__ff__ **and**

The man did hu__ff__ **and** pu__ff__.

ll

The

The bell

The bell fell

The bell fell on

The bell fell on the

The bell fell on the hill.

SS

The

The me<u>ss</u>

The me<u>ss</u> is

The me<u>ss</u> is on

The me<u>ss</u> is on the

The me<u>ss</u> is on the bed.

zz

Buzz,

Buzz, buzz

Buzz, buzz **went**

Buzz, buzz **went the**

Buzz, buzz **went the** big

Buzz, buzz **went the** big .

ACTIVITY

Double Letters

1. Look at the picture.
2. Circle the correct spelling of the word.
   (Remember the Double Letter Rule.)

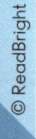

1	sel	sell
2	hat	hatt
3	fiz	fizz
4	puf	puff
5	ten	tenn
6	fuz	fuzz
7	log	logg
8	bil	bill
9	mes	mess

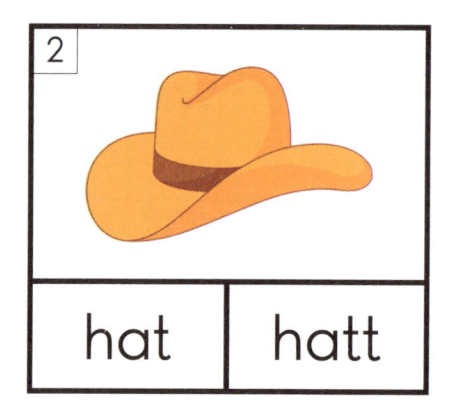

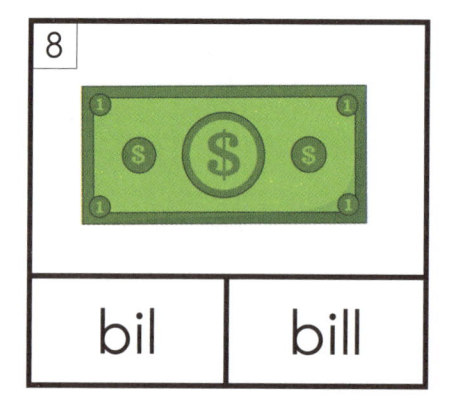

ACTIVITY

Double Letters

1. Look at the picture.
2. Write the correct letter or letters in the box to complete the word.
   (Remember the Double Letter Rule.)

1 be☐	2 po☐	3 hi☐
4 bi☐	5 do☐	6 me☐
7 ma☐	8 bu☐	9 pe☐

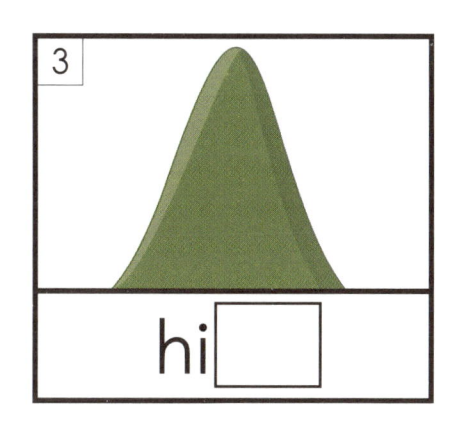

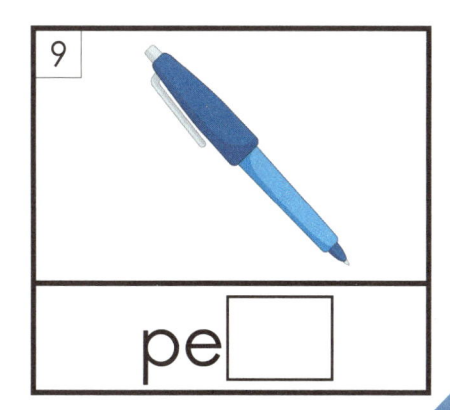

121

Phonics Skill: Double Letters

Pop Words: off   are   all

POP WORDS

off

1. I can get off the 🪜.
2. I can get off the 🧱.
3. I can get off the 🚚.
4. I can get off the 🛝.

are

5. The kids are on the hill.
6. The hens are on the hill.
7. The bugs are on the hill.
8. The vans are on the hill.

all

9. Are all the dolls wet?
10. All the dolls are wet.
11. Are all the dolls big?
12. All the dolls are big.

Pop Words: | off | are | all

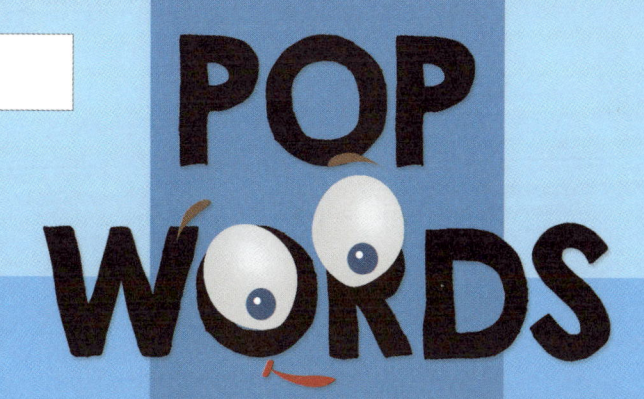

POP WORDS

1. all   off   are   she

2. he   do   went   off

3. was   are   me   to

4. we   for   all   be

Phonics Skill: **Double Letters**

Pop Words: off | are | all

POP WORDS

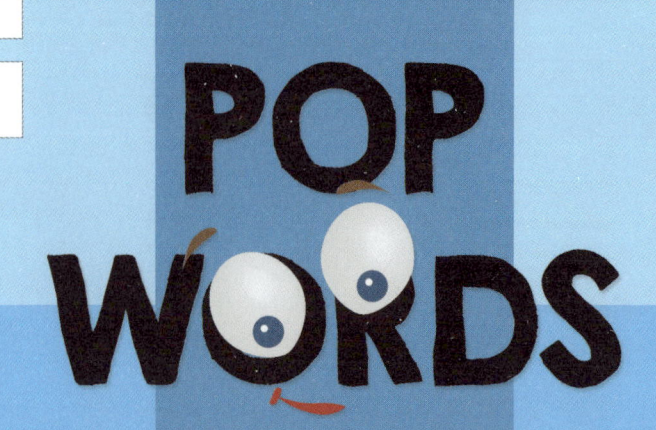

1. Read the sentence.
2. Circle the picture that matches the sentence.

1 The bugs are off the hill.		
2 All the kids fell off the bed.		
3 All the dolls are on the rug.		
4 The bell fell off the well.		
5 The bibs and hats are all wet.		

all

Read *all* /ȯl/ as the sound in 🏐.
(You can also teach *all* as a pop word.)

1. all   ball   tall

2. call   wall   mall

3. fall   hall   gall

all

The

The b<u>all</u>

The b<u>all</u> is

The b<u>all</u> is on

The b<u>all</u> is on the

The b<u>all</u> is on the t<u>all</u>

The b<u>all</u> is on the t<u>all</u> w<u>all</u>.

ACTIVITY

all

Draw a line from the word to the correct picture.

1. ball
2. fall
3. call
4. wall
5. tall

127

c or k?

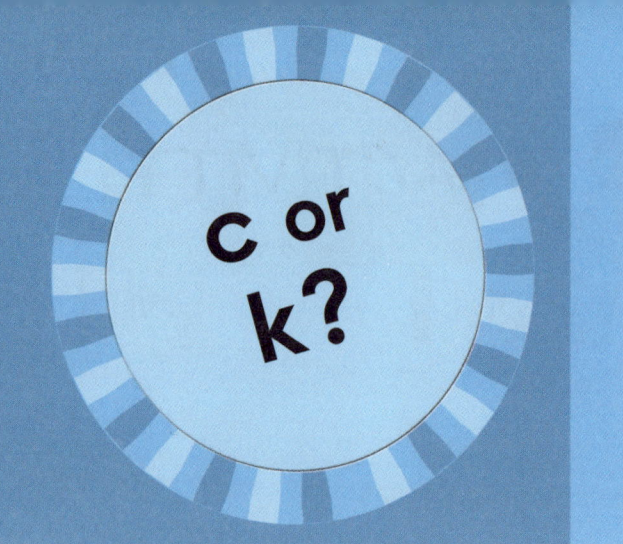

> In a one-syllable word, a /k/ beginning sound will be spelled with the letter **c**. It is spelled with the letter **k** only when the sound is followed by the letter *i*, *e*, or *y*.

c	a	1. can cat cap
	o	2. cot cop cob
	u	3. cup cud cuff
k	e / i	4. keg kit kiss

READ

ACTIVITY

c or k Spelling Rule

1. Look at the picture.
2. Write **c** or **k** in the box to complete the word.
   (Remember the *c* or *k* Spelling Rule.)

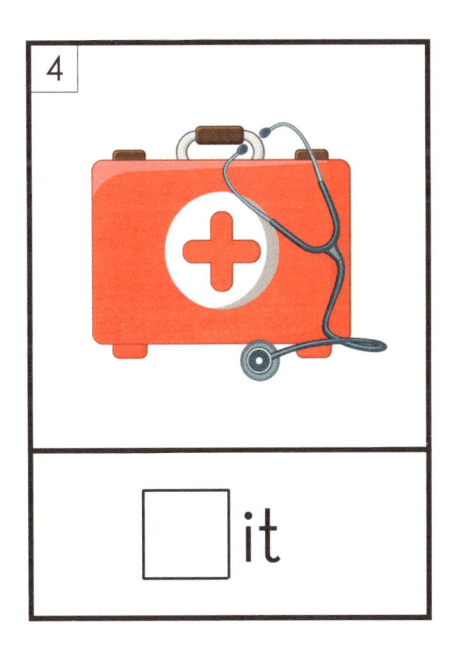

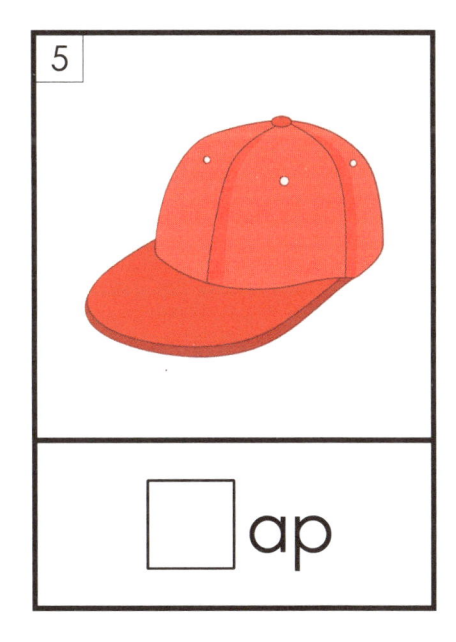

| 1 ☐up | 2 ☐id | 3 ☐at |
| 4 ☐it | 5 ☐ap | 6 ☐an |

ACTIVITY

c or k Spelling Rule

Write c or k in the box to complete the word.
(Remember the *c* or *k* Spelling Rule.)

1. ☐ab
2. ☐ob
3. ☐in
4. ☐ub
5. ☐id
6. ☐ud
7. ☐iss
8. ☐od
9. ☐eg
10. ☐ut
11. ☐it
12. ☐ot

Consonant Digraphs

Teaching Tip:

Consonant Digraphs: A consonant digraph is a combination of two consonants which form one sound.

To drill these sounds, have students say:
- each letter of the digraph
- the picture hint
- the sound it makes

For example: *c, k, kick, /k/*

Picture hints are found on top of the page when the digraph is first introduced.
These pictures correspond to the picture hints on the *ReadBright More Marvelous Hints* flashcards.

Consider digraphs to be like a single consonant in a *Kid in the Middle* (CVC) word. The center vowel sounds the same whether it is surrounded by single consonants or digraphs. Therefore, words with digraphs should be classified as *Kid in the Middle* words.

ck

ck   kick   /k/

1. back   kick   neck
2. dock   luck   tick
3. jack   deck   rock
4. suck   pick   tack
5. lock   rack   tuck

Digraphs

ck

MARK THE WORD

1. <u>Underline</u> the digraph **ck**.
2. Say the sound.
3. Read the word.

1. la<u>ck</u>   peck   mock   lick

2. duck   sack   wick   sock

nonsense words

3. dack   meck   wuck   jick

4. zock   huck   vick   yeck

WRITE

134

ck

The

The si<u>ck</u>

The si<u>ck</u> man

The si<u>ck</u> man **has**

The si<u>ck</u> man **has a**

The si<u>ck</u> man **has a** pop

The si<u>ck</u> man **has a** pop **to**

The si<u>ck</u> man **has a** pop **to** li<u>ck</u>.

ACTIVITY

ck

1. Look at the picture.
2. Circle the word that matches the picture.

1	deck
	neck
	wick

2	luck
	lock
	lick

3	pick
	mock
	tuck

4	tick
	suck
	duck

5	rock
	sock
	rack

6	lack
	sick
	sack

7	jack
	pack
	peck

8	dock
	kick
	back

ACTIVITY

ck

1. Read the question.
2. Put a ✓ next to the correct answer.

1 Can a duck fix a fan?	☐ yes	☐ no
2 Can a cat lick a neck?	☐ yes	☐ no
3 Can a rock get sick?	☐ yes	☐ no
4 Can a sack kick a back?	☐ yes	☐ no
5 Can a kid pack a bag?	☐ yes	☐ no
6 Can a sock lick?	☐ yes	☐ no
7 Can you pick up a lock?	☐ yes	☐ no

Phonics Skill: ck

Pop Words: no go so

POP WORDS

1. I have no socks.
2. I have no rocks.
3. I have no ducks.
4. I have no locks.

5. I go get a sock.
6. I go get a rock.
7. I go get a duck.
8. I go get a lock.

9. The sock is so wet.
10. The rock is so hot.
11. The duck is so tall.
12. The lock is so big.

Pop Words: | no | go | so |

POP WORDS

1. so   no   go
2. he   all   are
3. go   she   we
4. me   for   off
5. no   be   so

Pop Words:

| no | go | so |

POP WORDS

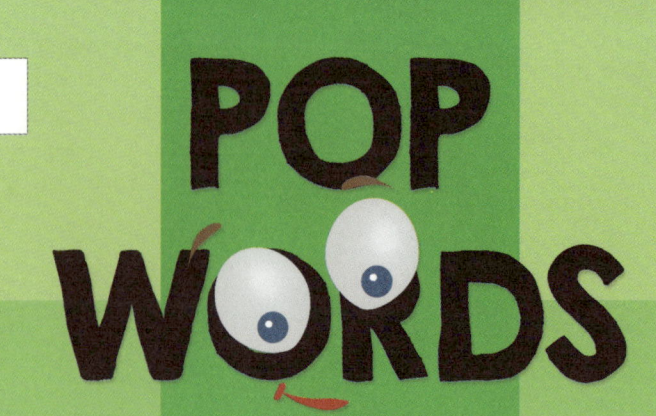

1. Read the pop word in the shaded box.
2. Circle the same pop word in the row next to it.

1 so	is	on	so	no
2 no	on	no	of	so
3 go	so	do	no	go

Unscramble the pop word.
Use the word box if you need a hint.

1 o, g	__ __
2 o, s	__ __
3 o, n	__ __

Word Box

so   no

go

sh

sh   ship   /sh/

1. shed — ship — shop
2. sash — shag — bash
3. wish — mesh — gush
4. dish — rash — lush
5. shell — shock — shack

Digraphs

sh

MARK THE WORD

1. <u>Underline</u> the digraph **sh**.
2. Say the sound.
3. Read the word.

1. hu<u>sh</u>   fi<u>sh</u>   <u>sh</u>ot   la<u>sh</u>

2. ru<u>sh</u>   <u>sh</u>ut   ma<u>sh</u>   <u>sh</u>un

nonsense words

3. ni<u>sh</u>   za<u>sh</u>   <u>sh</u>ap   <u>sh</u>ib

4. <u>sh</u>em   de<u>sh</u>   <u>sh</u>uff   vo<u>sh</u>

WRITE

sh

The

The fish

The fish is

The fish is on

The fish is on the

The fish is on the ship.

ACTIVITY

sh

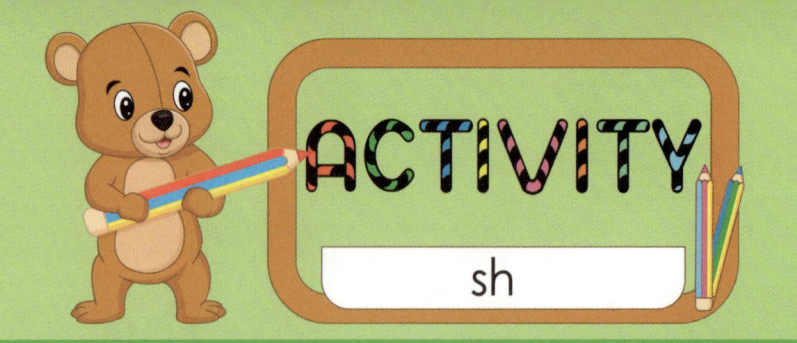

1. Look at the picture.
2. Circle the word that matches the picture.

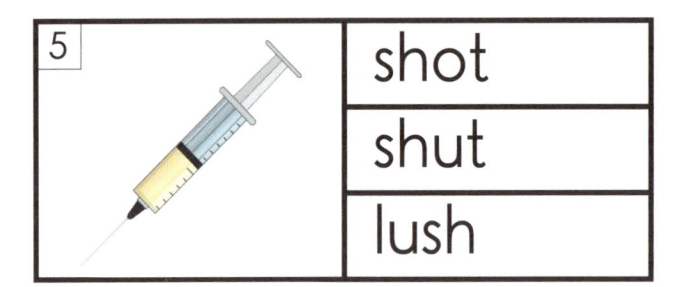

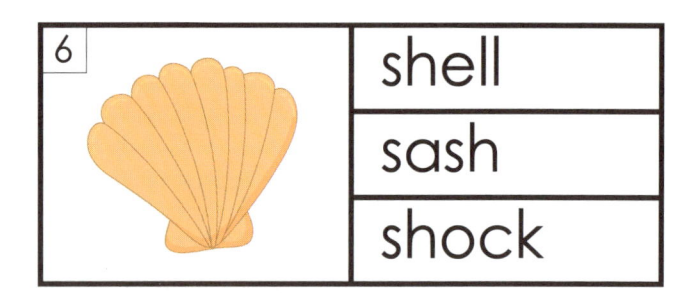

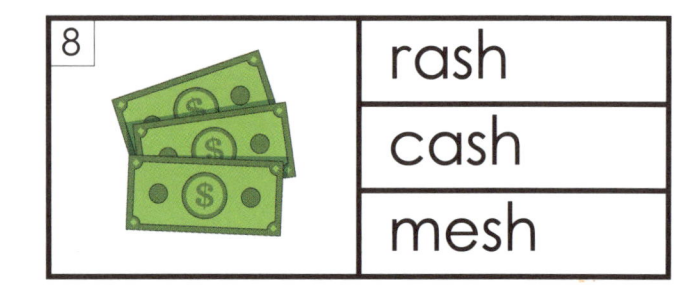

1	wish / fish / shop	2	shag / dash / ship
3	shed / bash / dish	4	shack / rush / gash
5	shot / shut / lush	6	shell / sash / shock
7	hush / shun / shop	8	rash / cash / mesh

ACTIVITY

sh

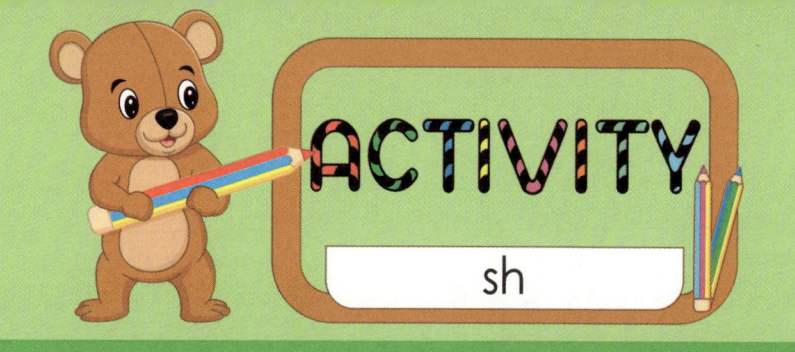

1. Read the question.
2. Put a ✓ next to the correct answer.

1 Is a ship big?	☐ yes ☐ no
2 Do you wish for a cat?	☐ yes ☐ no
3 Is a shed sad?	☐ yes ☐ no
4 Can a man rush?	☐ yes ☐ no
5 Can a shell mop?	☐ yes ☐ no
6 Do bugs shop?	☐ yes ☐ no
7 Can a fish hop?	☐ yes ☐ no

s/sh

	s	sh	s	sh
1.	sip	ship	sop	shop
2.	sag	shag	sun	shun
3.	sock	shock	sack	shack
4.	sell	shell	mass	mash

Note to Teachers: Teach these words by reading across the grid (*sip, ship; sop, shop*). This will emphasize the contrast between the *s* sound and the digraph *sh*.

READ

ACTIVITY
s / sh

1. Look at the picture.
2. Write [s] or [sh] in the box to complete the word.

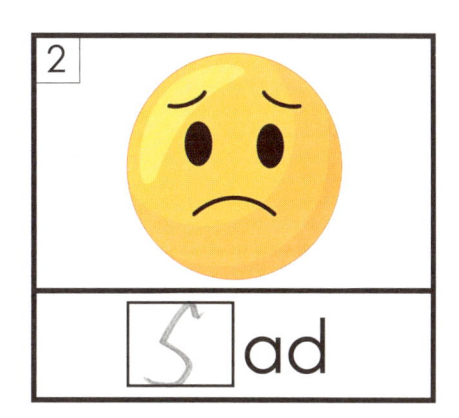

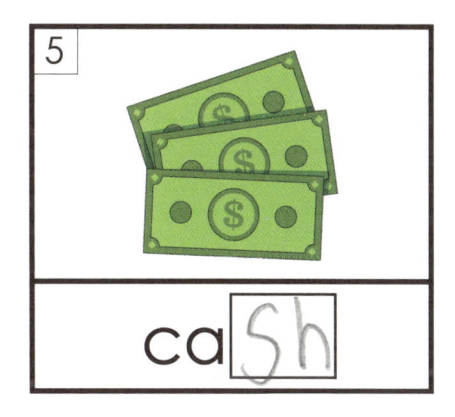

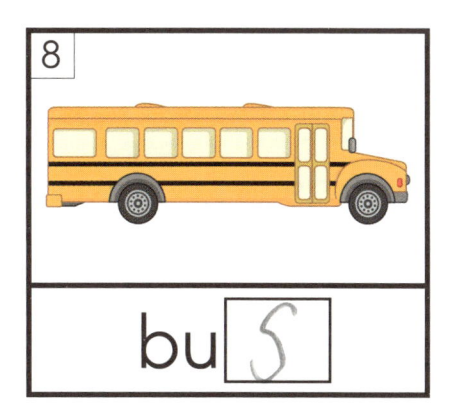

1	2	3
[Sh]ell	[S]ad	di[sh]

4	5	6
[S]ock	ca[sh]	[S]ip

7	8	9
ma[sh]	bu[s]	ru[sh]

Phonics Skill: sh

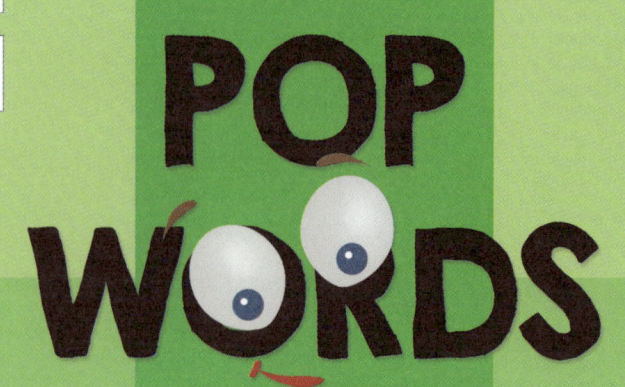

Pop Words: her   said   as

POP WORDS

1. It is her ship.
2. It is her dish.
3. It is her shell.
4. It is her fish.

5. She said her ship is big.
6. She said her dish is big.
7. She said her shell is big.
8. She said her fish is big.

9. The ship is as big as her bag.
10. The dish is as big as her pan.
11. The shell is as big as her cup.
12. The fish is as big as her can.

Pop Words: | her | said | as |

POP WORDS

1. her   as   said

2. she   me   are

3. be   said   no

4. he   her   we

5. so   go   as

Pop Words: | her | said | as |

POP WORDS

1. Read the pop word in the shaded box.
2. Circle the same pop word in the row next to it.

1	as	as	has	so	his
2	her	the	her	he	she
3	said	she	so	said	as

Unscramble the pop word.
Use the word box if you need a hint.

1	s, a	__ __
2	r, h, e	__ __ __
3	a, d, s, i	__ __ __ __

Word Box

her	as
said	

150

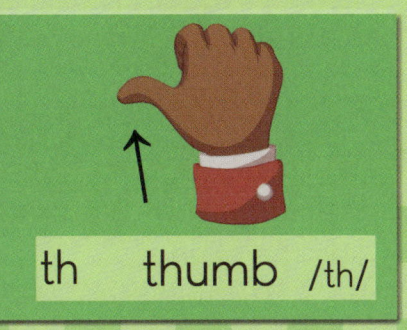

th

th   thumb   /th/

1. thud   thin   thick

2. bath   math   with

3. that   than   them

4. this   then   thus

Note to Teachers:
The digraph **th** has two sounds:
1. /th/ as in the word ba**th**, and
2. /th/ as in the word **th**en.
If students don't know which sound to use, tell them to try both options and choose the one that sounds "right."

Digraphs

th

MARK THE WORD

1. <u>Underline</u> the digraph **th**.
2. Say the sound.
3. Read the word.

1. wi__th__   thin   that   this

2. pa__th__   __th__em   __th__ug   ba__th__

nonsense words

3. __th__ip   na__th__   __th__eg   bi__th__

4. __th__et   __th__un   ga__th__   __th__im

WRITE

th

Sam

Sam did

Sam did ma<u>th</u>

Sam did ma<u>th</u> in

Sam did ma<u>th</u> in **the**

Sam did ma<u>th</u> in **the** ba<u>th</u>.

ACTIVITY
th

1. Look at the picture.
2. Circle the word that matches the picture.

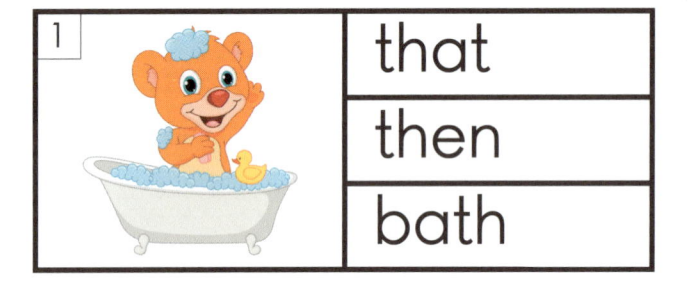

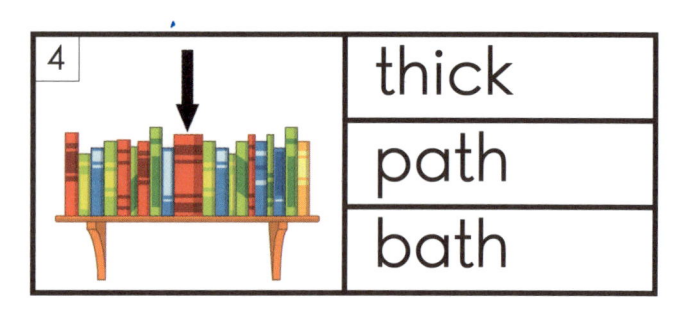

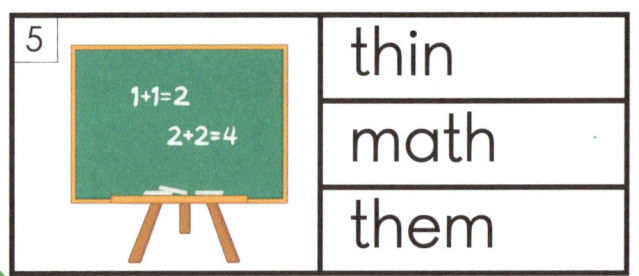

1	that
	then
	bath

	thud
	with
	path

3	thin
	thug
	than

4	thick
	path
	bath

5	thin
	math
	them

6	math
	them
	thus

ACTIVITY

th

1. Read the question.
2. Put a ✓ next to the correct answer.

1. Can a kid have a bath?	☑ yes ☐ no
2. Can a duck do math?	☐ yes ☑ no
3. Can men run with a kid?	☑ yes ☐ no
4. Is a thin man fat?	☐ yes ☑ no
5. Can fish hop on a path?	☐ yes ☑ no
6. Do you have a thick pad?	☐ yes ☑ no
7. Can kids sit and then dig?	☑ yes ☐ no

t/th

	t	th	t	th
1.	ten	then	tin	thin
2.	tug	thug	tan	than
3.	tick	thick	mat	math
4.	bat	bath	pat	path

Note to Teachers: Teach these words by reading across the grid (*ten, then; tin, thin*). This will emphasize the contrast between the *t* sound and the digraph *th*.

READ

ACTIVITY
t / th

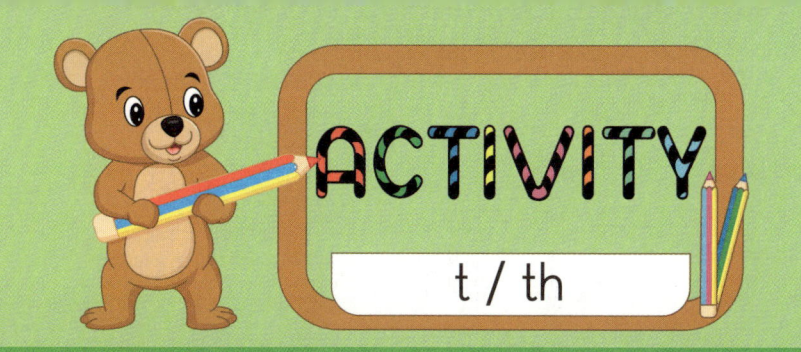

1. Look at the picture.
2. Write **t** or **th** in the box to complete the word.

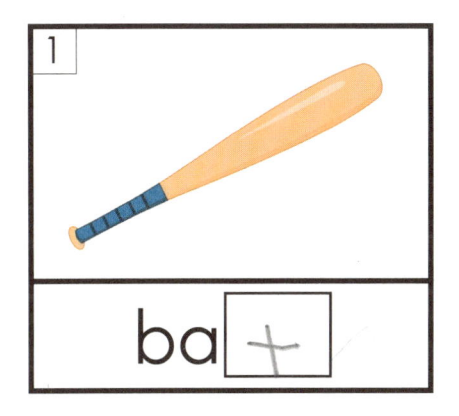

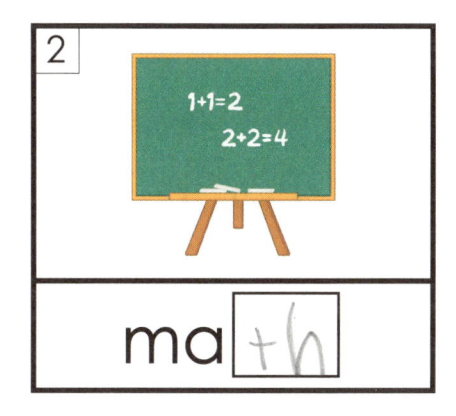

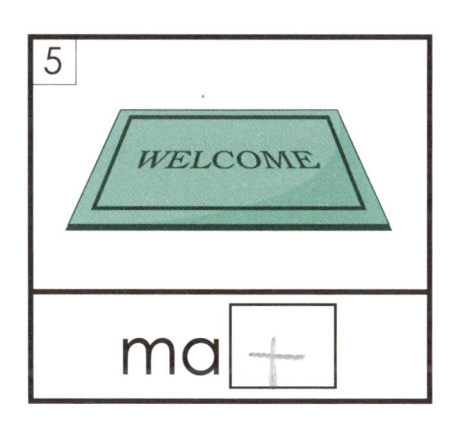

1. ba**t**	2. ma**th**	3. **t**en
4. ba**th**	5. ma**t**	6. **th**ick
7. si**t**	8. pa**th**	9. ha**t**

ck • sh th

1. sack   fish   them

2. shed   thin   lock

3. path   lick   mesh

4. back   cash   with

5. shock   shell   thick

READ review

ACTIVITY
ck · sh · th

1. Read the sentence.
2. Look at the picture.
3. Circle the ✓ if the picture matches the sentence.
   Circle the ✗ if the picture does not match the sentence.

1. A duck has a sock.		✓
2. The man is thin.		✓
3. The fish are in the shop.		✗
4. This is a big lock.		✗
5. The cat can lick the ball.		✓
6. The kid got a rash.		✗

Phonics Skill: th

Pop Words: this that with they

POP WORDS

1. Is this a path?
2. This is a path.
3. Is this a bath?
4. This is a bath.

5. Is that a man on the path?
6. That is a man on the path.
7. Is that a kid in the bath?
8. That is a kid in the bath.

9. Is the man with a pal?
10. The man is with a pal.
11. Is the kid with a duck?
12. The kid is with a duck.

13. Do they have fun on the path?
14. They have fun on the path.
15. Do they have fun in the bath?
16. They have fun in the bath.

Pop Words: | this | that | with | they

POP WORDS

1. that — this — they
2. with — as — her
3. so — that — go
4. this — said — they
5. no — with — he

Pop Words: | this | that | with | they |

POP WORDS

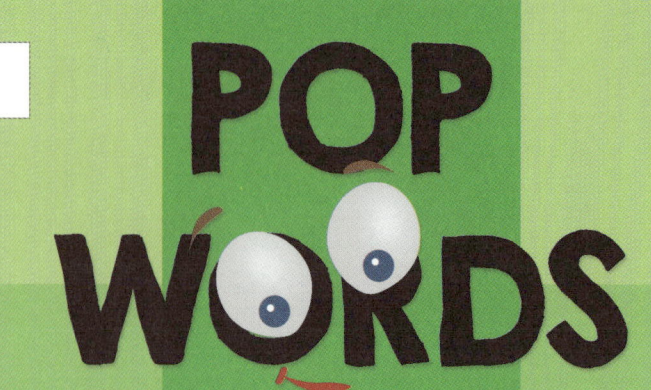

1. Read the pop word in the shaded box.
2. Circle the same pop word in the row next to it.

1	with	was	with	the	went
2	they	the	that	they	with
3	this	is	the	that	this
4	that	the	they	this	that

Unscramble the pop word.
Use the word box if you need a hint.

1	h, e, y, t	__ __ __ __
2	h, a, t, t	__ __ __ __
3	h, w, i, t	__ __ __ __

Word Box

with   they

that

ch

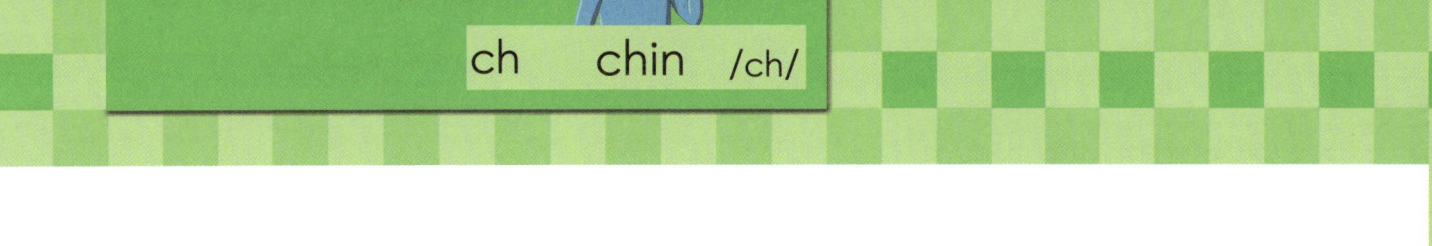

ch   chin   /ch/

1. chat   chin   chop
2. chug   chap   chip
3. chock   chum   check
4. chess   chick   chill
5. such   rich   much

Digraphs

ch

MARK THE WORD

1. Underline the digraph **ch**.
2. Say the sound.
3. Read the word.

1. such   chop   chill   chum

2. chat   chug   much   chap

nonsense words

3. zich   chiff   chud   chab

4. chot   chass   vuch   chen

WRITE

164

ch

The

The chick

The chick is

The chick is on

The chick is on his

The chick is on his chin.

ACTIVITY

ch

1. Look at the picture.
2. Circle the word that matches the picture.

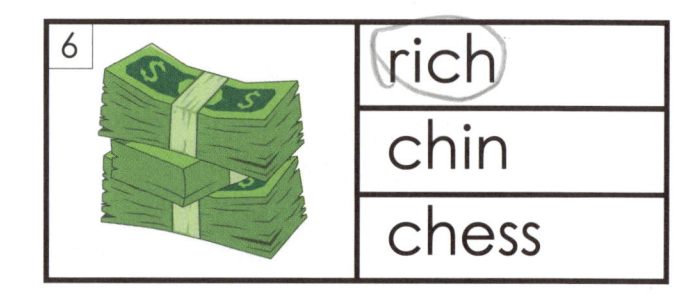

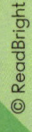

1	chat
	(chip)
	rich

2	chip
	chill
	(chick)

3	such
	(chop)
	chug

4	chock
	chick
	(check)

5	check
	(chess)
	chap

6	(rich)
	chin
	chess

166

ACTIVITY
ch

1. Read the question.
2. Put a ✓ next to the correct answer.

1 Is a chick red?	☐ yes	☑ no
2 Will you chop a bed?	☐ yes	☑ no
3 Do you have a chin?	☑ yes	☐ no
4 Can a cat chat?	☐ yes	☑ no
5 Can a chip nap?	☐ yes	☑ no
6 Do you have a chess set?	☐ yes	☑ no
7 Is a ship rich?	☐ yes	☑ no

c/ch

	c	ch	c	ch
1.	cop	chop	cap	chap
2.	cat	chat	cub	chub
3.	can	chip	cot	chin
4.	cob	chug	cut	chess

Note to Teachers: Teach these words by reading across the grid (*cop, chop; cap, chap*). This will emphasize the contrast between the *c* sound and the digraph *ch*.

READ

ACTIVITY
c / ch / ck

1. Look at the picture.
2. Write c, ch, or ck in the box to complete the word.

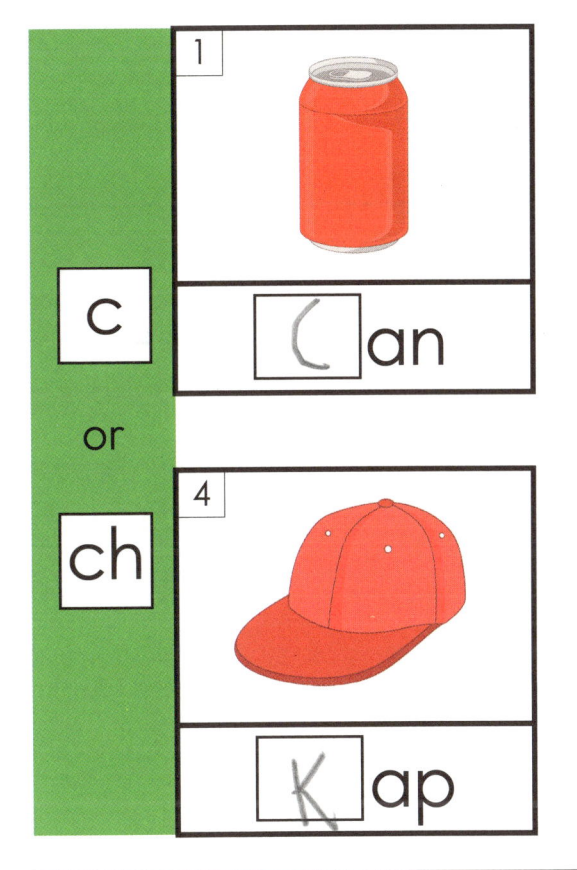

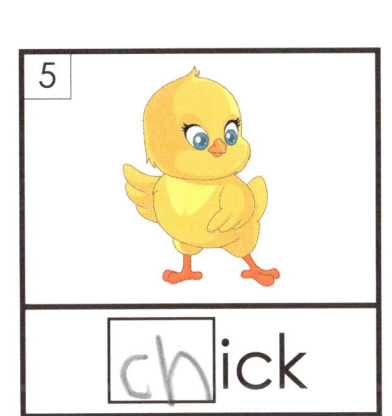

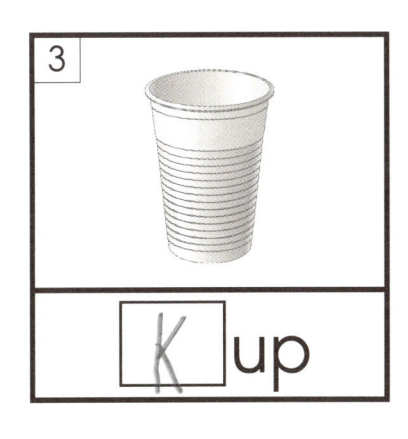

c or ch

1. [can] — **c**an
2. [chin] — **ch**in
3. [cup] — **k**up
4. [cap] — **k**ap
5. [chick] — **ch**ick
6. [chip] — **ch**ip

ck or ch

7. [back] — ba**k**
8. [rich] — ri**ch**
9. [sick] — si**k**

ACTIVITY
sh / ch

Circle the best word for the sentence.

1. He got a [shot] / chot .

2. I can go on a big [ship] / chip .

3. A red mop is in the [shed] / ched .

4. I will sheck / [check] the pot.

5. The kids will [shop] / chop for caps.

6. Did you [shut] / chut the box?

7. This is sush / [such] a big rock.

ck·sh
th·ch

1. rich   that   sock

2. bath   dash   chill

3. shot   wick   thud

4. rash   check   then

5. shack   hush   chick

ACTIVITY
ck · sh · th · ch

1. Read the sentence.
2. Look at the picture.
3. Circle the ✓ if the picture matches the sentence.
   Circle the ✗ if the picture does not match the sentence.

1	The fish is on the dish.		✓
2	The bath is hot.		✓
3	The kids can pack a sack.		✓
4	The rich man has a hat.		✗
5	She can do math.		✓
6	The hen is with the chicks.		✓

Phonics Skill: ch

Pop Words: by | from | my

POP WORDS

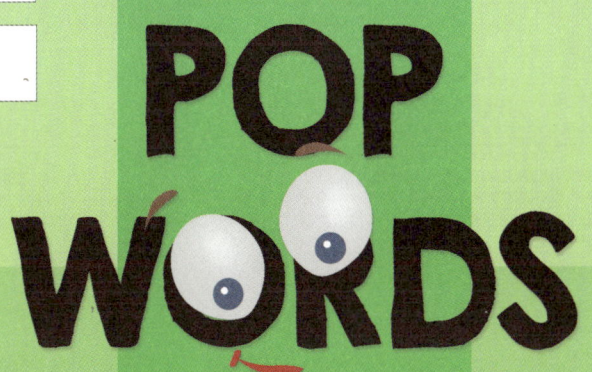

1. I pass by the shop.
2. I pass by the man.
3. I pass by the kid.
4. I pass by the van.

5. I get a chick from the shop.
6. I get a hat from the man.
7. I get a chip from the kid.
8. I get a bat from the van.

9. This is my chick.
10. This is my hat.
11. This is my chip.
12. This is my bat.

Pop Words: | by | from | my |

POP WORDS

1. by my from

2. that her they

3. so said my

4. with by this

5. from no as

Pop Words: | by | from | my |

POP WORDS

1. Read the pop word in the shaded box.
2. Circle the same pop word in the row next to it.

1 by	be	by	all	no
2 my	my	me	they	we
3 from	for	with	down	from

Unscramble the pop word.
Use the word box if you need a hint.

1 f, m, o, r	__ __ __ __
2 y, m	__ __
3 y, b	__ __

Word Box

| by | my |
| from | |

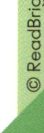

175

wh

wh whale /w/

1. whit   whip   whim

2. whiz   whack   whiff

3. when   which   whet

nonsense words

4. whid   wheck   whab

5. whess   wheff   whiss

READ

wh

When

When will

When will **the**

When will **the** cat

When will **the** cat nap?

Phonics Skill wh

Pop Words: what when which how ??

POP WORDS

1. What can a cat do?
2. What can a kid do?
3. What can a dog do?
4. What can a man do?

5. When do cats nap?
6. When do kids lick?
7. When do dogs dig?
8. When do men kick?

9. Which cat can nap?
10. Which kid can lick?
11. Which dog can dig?
12. Which man can kick?

13. How well can you nap?
14. How well can you lick?
15. How well can you dig?
16. How well can you kick?

Pop Words: what | when | which | how

POP WORDS

1. what   which   when
2. how   that   what
3. as   they   her
4. this   which   with
5. when   said   how

Pop Words: | what | when | which | how |

POP WORDS

1. Read the pop word in the shaded box.
2. Circle the same pop word in the row next to it.

1	what	when	what	that	the
2	which	what	which	when	with
3	when	that	they	when	what
4	how	his	has	he	how

Unscramble the pop word.
Use the word box if you need a hint.

1	w, o, h	__ __ __
2	e, h, n, w	__ __ __ __
3	a, h, w, t	__ __ __ __
4	c, w, i, h, h	__ __ __ __ __

Word Box

which	how
what	when

180

qu

qu   queen   /kw/

1. quiz   quack   quit
2. quick   quill   quip

nonsense words

3. quan   queck   quig
4. queg   quib   quop
5. quix   quess   quin

Digraphs

wh
qu

MARK THE WORD

1. Underline the digraphs **wh** and **qu**.
2. Say the sound.
3. Read the word.

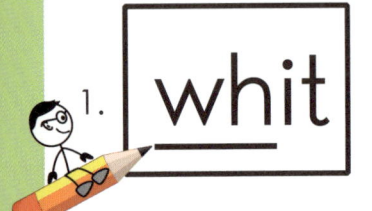

1. <u>wh</u>it   when   whiz   whiff

2. quill   quiz   quit   quell

nonsense words

3. wheg   whab   whem   whid

4. quiss   quem   quap   quet

WRITE

qu

"Quack,

"Quack, quack,"

"Quack, quack," **said**

"Quack, quack," **said the**

"Quack, quack," **said the** duck.

ACTIVITY
wh · qu

1. Look at the picture.
2. Circle the word that matches the picture.

1	quack / whack / quiz
2	quip / whip / quit
3	quill / quick / whip
4	quick / quack / quill

1. Read the question.
2. Put a ✓ next to the correct answer.

1	Can a duck quack?	☐ yes	☐ no
2	Can a kid have a quick nap?	☐ yes	☐ no
3	Will you whip a fan?	☐ yes	☐ no
4	Can you quit a job?	☐ yes	☐ no

Digraphs

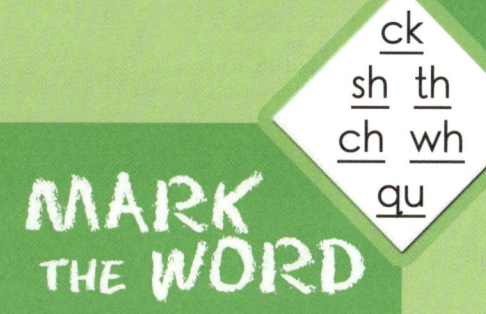

ck
sh th
ch wh
qu

MARK THE WORD

1. Underline the digraph.
2. Say the sound.
3. Read the word.

1. pi<u>ck</u>   whim   much   quit

2. than   lush   whiff   shag

3. whip   neck   math   sash

4. quill   duck   chip   quiz

ACTIVITY
Digraphs

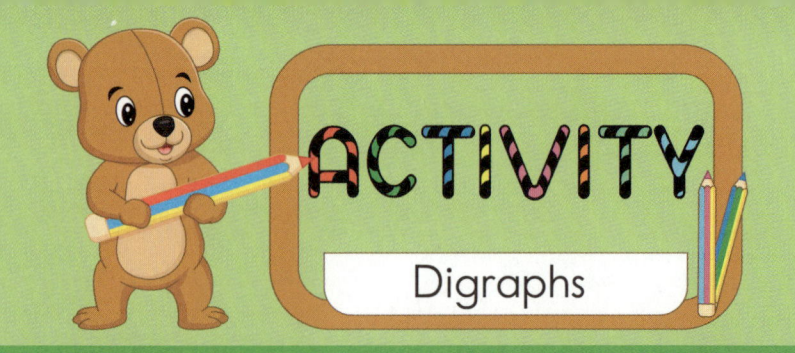

1. Read the sentence.
2. Look at the picture.
3. Circle the ✓ if the picture matches the sentence.
   Circle the ✗ if the picture does not match the sentence.

1 The shell is in the shed.		✓ ✗
2 Chips are on the chess set.		✓ ✗
3 The bug is on the path.		✓ ✗
4 The man has a whip.		✓ ✗
5 The box has a lock.		✓ ✗
6 The duck can quack.		✓ ✗

ACTIVITY
Digraphs

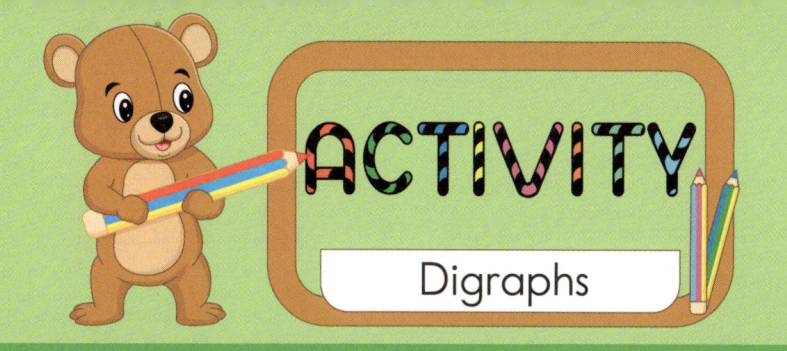

1. Say the name of the picture.
2. Circle the digraph that makes the beginning sound of the word.

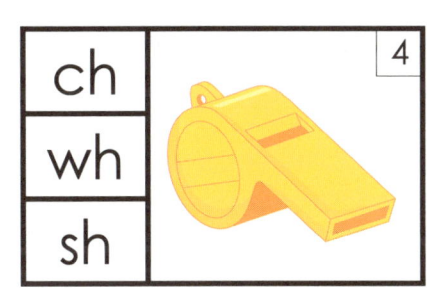

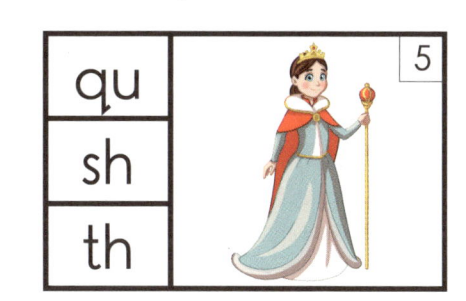

| 1 | th / sh / (ch) | 2 | ch / (sh) / th | 3 | wh / (th) / ch |
| 4 | ch / wh / sh | 5 | qu / sh / th | 6 | wh / qu / ch |

1. Say the name of the picture.
2. Circle the digraph that makes the ending sound of the word.

| 1 | ch / ck / sh | 2 | th / sh / ch | 3 | ck / ch / th |

ACTIVITY
Digraphs

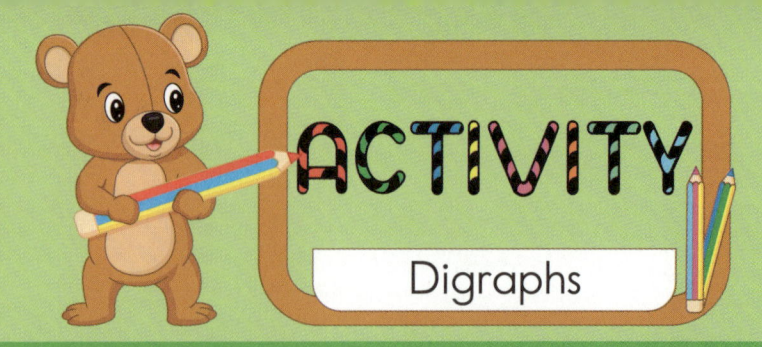

1. Say the name of the picture.
2. Look at the pairs of boxes beside each picture.
3. Shade in the box in each pair that has the letter or letters in the word.
4. Write the word in the empty box at the end of the row.

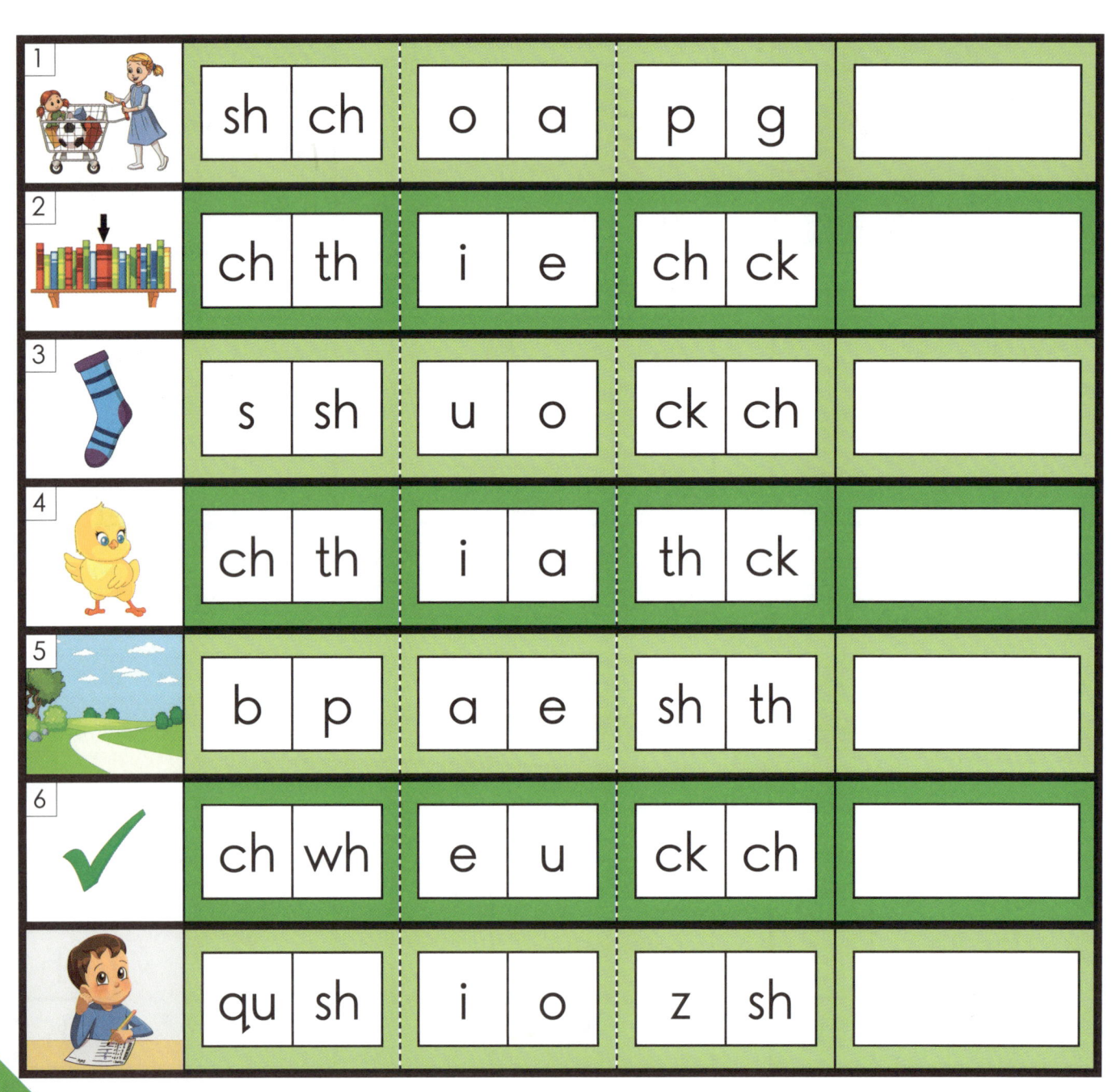

1		sh	ch	o	a	p	g	
2		ch	th	i	e	ch	ck	
3		s	sh	u	o	ck	ch	
4		ch	th	i	a	th	ck	
5		b	p	a	e	sh	th	
6		ch	wh	e	u	ck	ch	
7		qu	sh	i	o	z	sh	

188

ACTIVITY
Digraphs

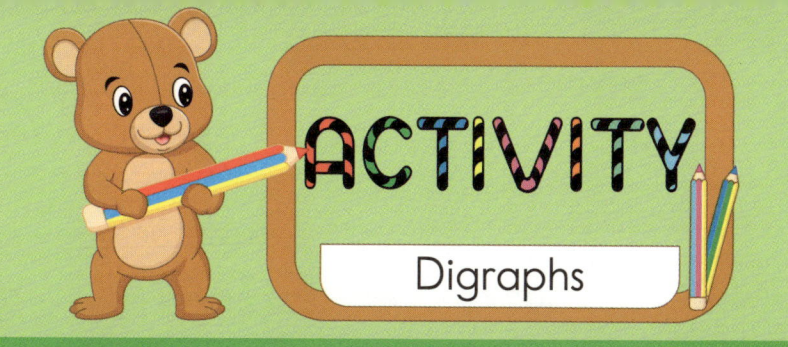

1. Say the name of the picture.
2. Draw a line from the picture to the digraph that makes the beginning sound of the word.

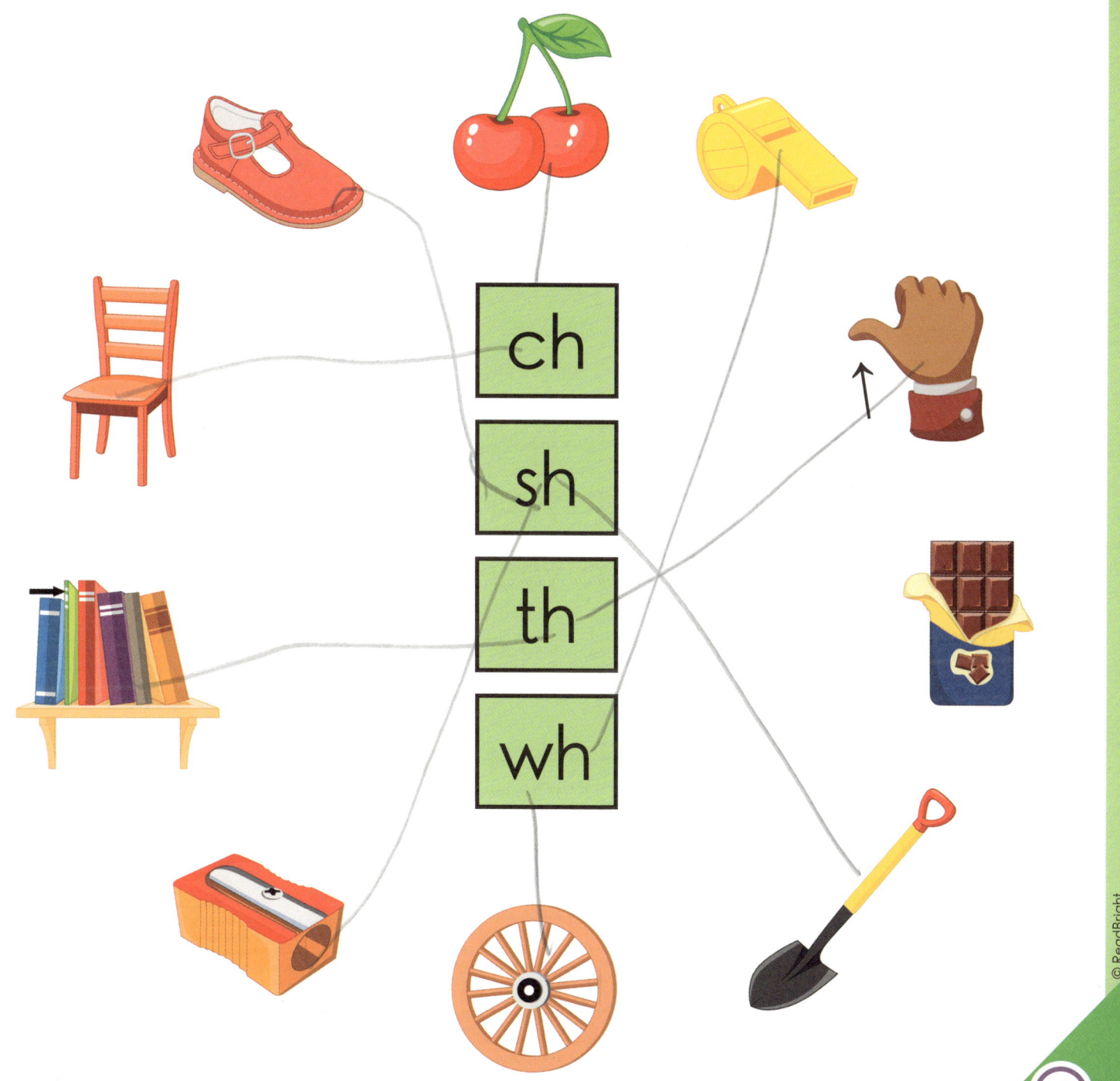

- ch
- sh
- th
- wh

189

Phonics Skill: qu

Pop Words: or   your   see

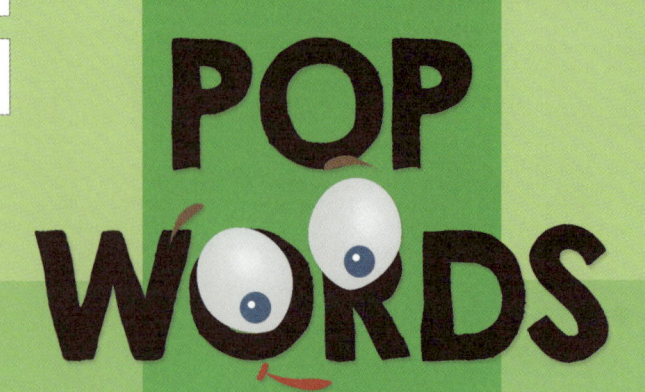

POP WORDS

1. Do you have a rug or a mug?
2. Do you have a mat or a hat?
3. Do you have a dish or a fish?
4. Do you have a box or a fox?

5. Quick! Tell me! Is that your rug?
6. Quick! Tell me! Is that your mat?
7. Quick! Tell me! Is that your dish?
8. Quick! Tell me! Is that your box?

9. I see a mug on the rug.
10. I see a hat on the mat.
11. I see a fish on the dish.
12. I see a fox on the box.

Pop Words: | or | your | see

POP WORDS

1. or — your — see
2. with — which — or
3. what — when — your
4. by — from — they
5. see — my — how

Pop Words:

| or | your | see |

POP WORDS

1. Read the pop word in the shaded box.
2. Circle the same pop word in the row next to it.

#					
1	or	no	her	(or)	do
2	your	you	(your)	her	or
3	see	she	as	was	(see)

Unscramble the pop word.
Use the word box if you need a hint.

#		
1	e, s, e	see
2	r, o	or
3	u, o, r, y	your

Word Box

or   see

your

Special Rules

Special Rules

S symbols

Symbols are markings that have meaning. Punctuation marks are symbols that make the meaning of written words more clear.

194

A period (.) is a dot that comes at the end of a sentence. Tell students to stop for a moment when they reach a period.

A question mark (?) comes at the end of a question. Tell students to use the voice they use for asking when reading a sentence with a question mark.

1. I have a box.
2. What is in it?
3. Can you tell me?
4. It is red.
5. It is big.
6. Can it go up and down?
7. Yes, it can.
8. Is it a ball?
9. Yes, it is a ball.

ACTIVITY

. ?

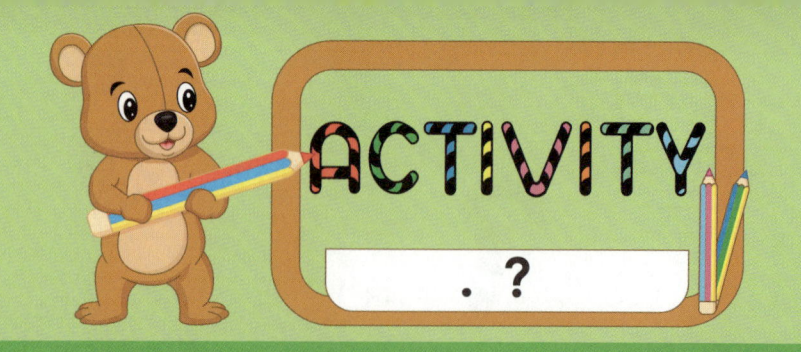

1. Read the sentence.
2. Put the correct punctuation mark at the end of the sentence. Write a **.** or a **?**.

1. Can you run with me

2. Can we run to the hill

3. We will see if I will win

4. We will see if you will win

5. I can be so quick

6. Can you be quick

7. It will be fun to run with you

An **exclamation point** (!) comes at the end of a sentence that is full of strong feeling. Tell students to say this kind of sentence in an excited voice.

1. I see a fish.
2. It is all wet.
3. Go, fish, go!
4. The fish is up.
5. The fish is down.
6. Up!
7. Down!
8. What fun!

ACTIVITY

. ? !

1. Read the sentence.
2. Circle the correct punctuation mark.

1	What is in this pot	? !
2	I will check	? .
3	I pick up the lid	! .
4	Oh, no	? !
5	It is so hot	? !
6	I get all red	? .
7	What can I do	? .
8	I run to call Mom	? .

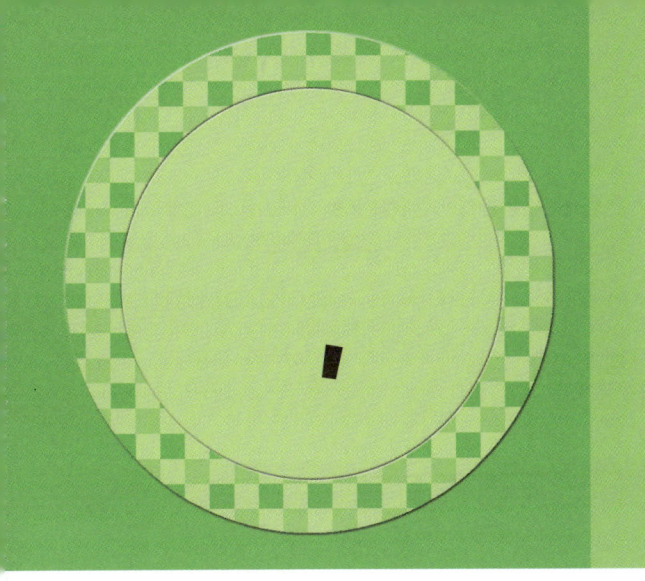

A comma (,) is used to separate words or groups of words in a sentence. For example, it is used after each item in a list (except the last one) when there are three or more items. Tell students to pause for a moment when they reach a comma.

1. Jack gets his bat, ball, and cap.

2. In a bag, he packs nuts, chips, and gum.

3. Jack has his bat, ball, cap, and bag.

4. He runs to his pals, Ned and Tom.

5. Jack, Ned, and Tom hit the ball with the bat.

6. On a mat, they have the nuts, chips, and gum.

7. Jack had fun with his bat, his ball, and his pals!

Quotation marks (" ") are used to show someone's exact words. They go before and after the person's words.

1. The man said, "I sell hats!"

2. "I will get a red hat," said Dad.

3. The man said, "I sell pots!"

4. "I will get a big pot," said Mom.

5. The man said, "I sell balls!"

6. "I will get a red ball," said Bob.

7. The man said, "I sell dolls!"

8. "I will get a big doll," said Meg.

ACTIVITY

1. Read the sentence.
2. Circle who is talking in each sentence.

1. "I can dig," said the man.
2. "I can run," said the kid.
3. "I can sit," said the hen.
4. "I can buzz," said the bug.
5. The chick said, "I can peck."
6. The duck said, "I can quack."
7. The dog said, "I can wag."
8. The cat said, "I can lick."

I can dig.

's

S An apostrophe s ('s) is used to show ownership. In the phrase "Ben's cap," the 's shows that the cap belongs to Ben.
To read words containing an 's:
- Cover the 's with your thumb.
- Read the base word.
- Lift your thumb.
- Read the whole word.

	This is Ted.
	This is Ted's ball.

1. Dad's van   Mom's pot

2. Jill's sock   Pam's bag

3. Rob's box   Meg's pad

4. the kid's bat   the man's pen

's

The

The doll's

The doll's hat

The doll's hat **is**

The doll's hat **is on**

The doll's hat **is on the**

The doll's hat **is on the** kid's

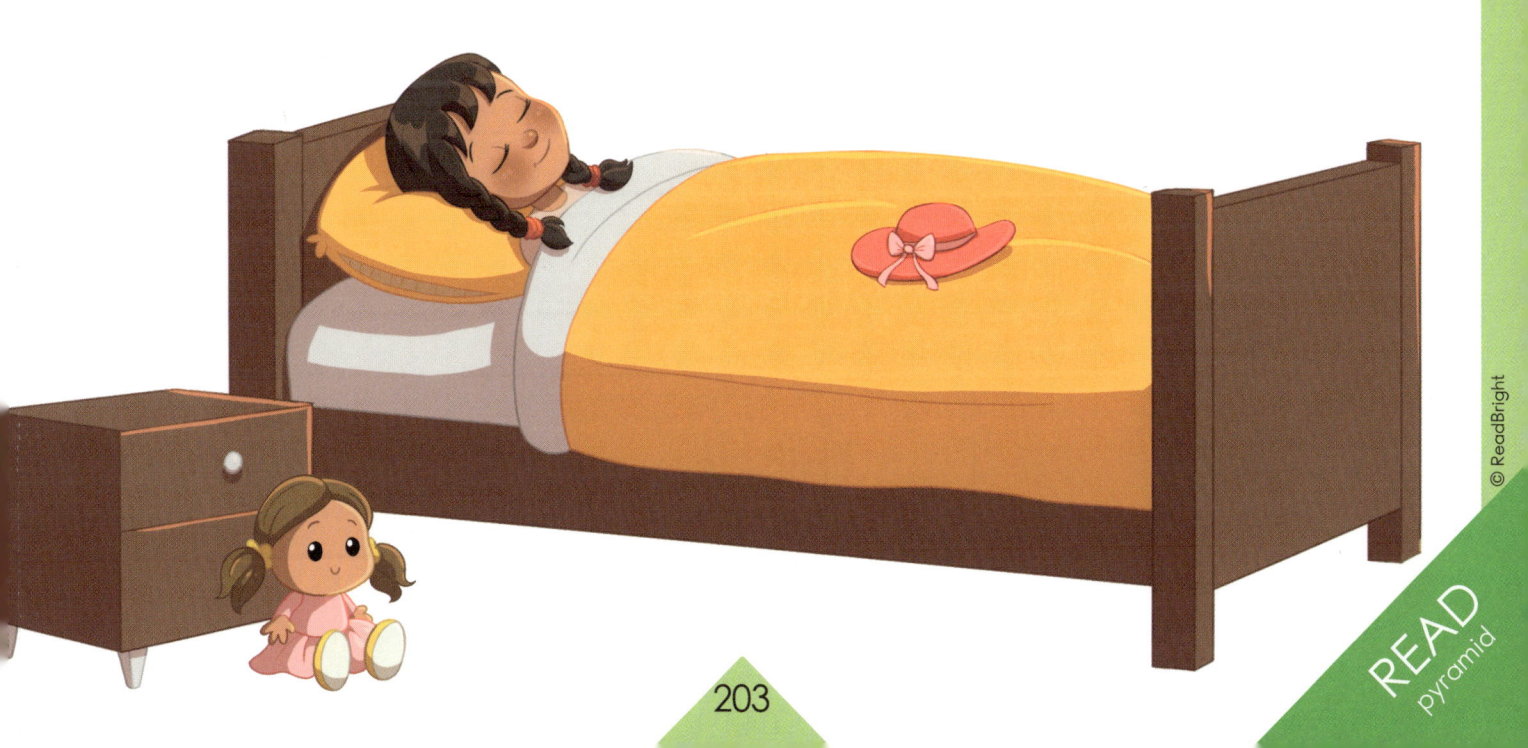

The doll's hat **is on the** kid's bed.

ACTIVITY

's

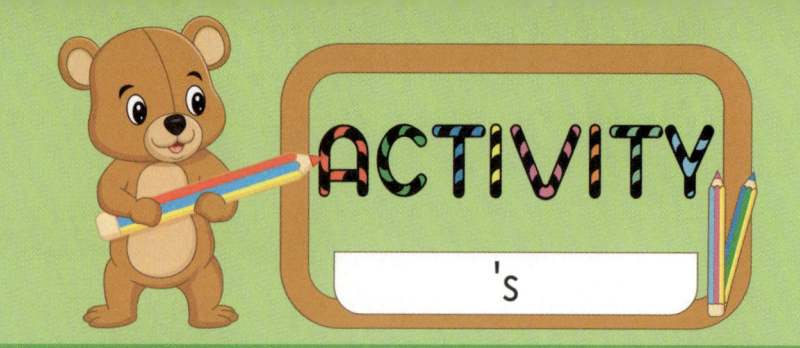

1. Look at a hat below. Then look at the people in the picture.
2. Find the hat's owner. Write his name on the line.
3. Write an 's on the next line to complete the sentence.

Jim	Bob	Ben	Dan	Sam

1		This is _____ __ hat.
2		This is _____ __ hat.
3		This is _____ __ hat.
4		This is _____ __ hat.
5		This is _____ __ hat.

Blends

Teaching Tip:

BLENDS: A blend is a combination of two or more consonants, each making their own sound. Although these sounds are pronounced distinctly, they are "blended" into one sound.

- - - - - - - -

Consider consonant blends to be like a single consonant in a *Kid in the Middle* (CVC) word. The center vowel sounds the same whether it is surrounded by single consonants, digraphs, or consonant blends. Therefore, words with blends should be classified as *Kid in the Middle* words.

- - - - - - - -

Demonstrate the concept of blends using a toy drum set.* The drum set should have three drums: One large drum in the center and a small drum on each side. Choose a blend to illustrate the concept. (The following example features the *st* blend.) On the left small drum, write the letter *s*. On the right small drum, write the letter *t*. Say the /s/ sound and tap on the *s* drum with one drumstick. Then say the /t/ sound and tap on the *t* drum with another drumstick. Next, articulate the /st/ sound while tapping with both drumsticks on the middle drum. This demonstrates how the sounds are blended into one sound.

*Credits to: Malkie Weinberger, Ms.Ed

Blends

1. Drum your left pointer finger on the left drum while saying the letter sound.
2. Drum your right pointer finger on the right drum while saying the letter sound.
3. Drum with both pointer fingers on the middle drum while saying the blend sound.

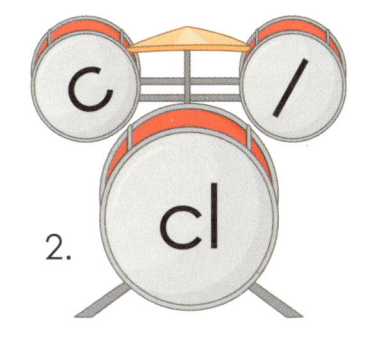

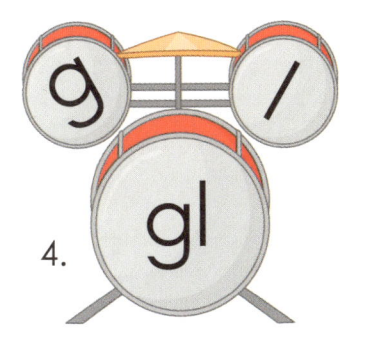

1. b / bl
2. c / cl
3. f / fl
4. g / gl
5. p / pl
6. s / sl

Blends

1.	bl	blot	bled	blob
2.	cl	clog	clan	clot
3.	fl	fled	flap	flip
4.	gl	glad	glum	glob
5.	pl	plan	plum	plus
6.	sl	slug	slid	slat

Beginning **drum**

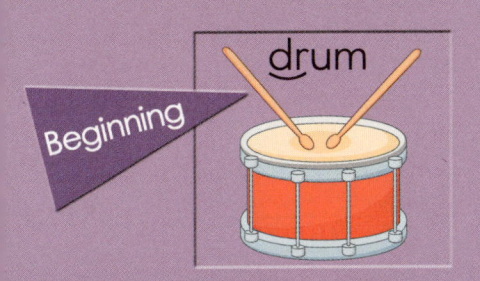

Blends

1.  br
2. 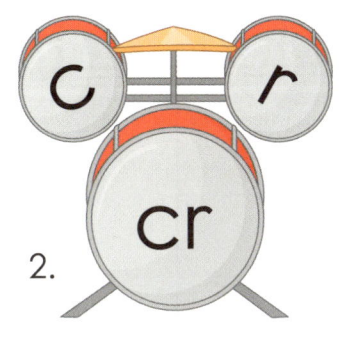 cr
3.  fr
4.  gr
5. 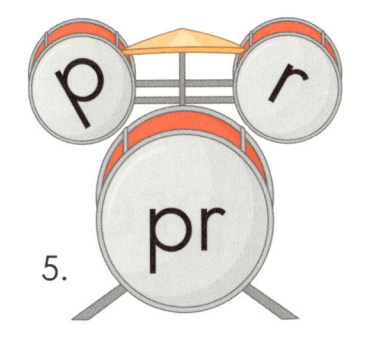 pr
6.  dr
7.  tr

209

Blends

1.	br	bran	brim	brass
2.	cr	cram	crop	crib
3.	fr	frog	fret	frill
4.	gr	grub	grip	grass
5.	pr	prim	prop	press

Blends

Beginning drum

s_

1. sc
2. sk
3. sm
4. sn
5. sp
6. st
7. sw

Blends

1.	sc	scan	scab	scuff
2.	sk	skit	skip	skill
3.	sn	snap	snip	sniff
4.	sp	spot	spun	spell
5.	st	stop	step	staff
6.	sw / sm	swim	swam	smell

Beginning Blends

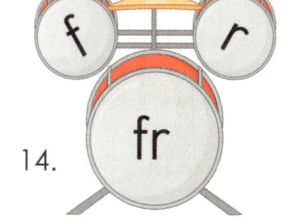

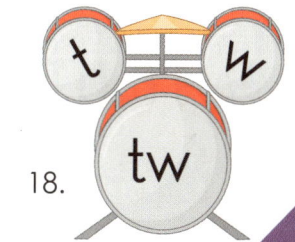

1. cl
2. br
3. sc
4. sw
5. gl
6. pr
7. fl
8. sk
9. cr
10. sl
11. sn
12. pl
13. st
14. fr
15. sp
16. gr
17. bl
18. tw

Blends

1. grill   skim   brass
2. slip   twin   spin
3. smug   bliss   stuff
4. class   swell   snug
5. fluff   pram   glass

Blends

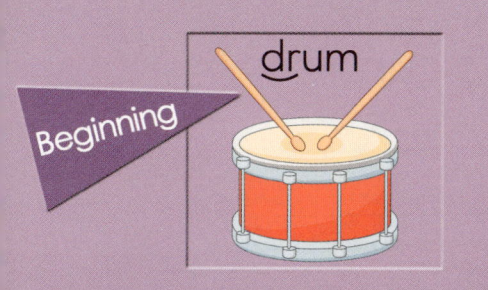

1. blush   brush   plush

2. snack   block   stuck

3. smock   smash   crack

4. flash   click   fresh

5. shred   thrill   thrash

Blends

MARK THE WORD

drum

1. Draw a ‿ under the blend.
2. Say the sound.
3. Read the word.

1. slit — snag — brag — flax

2. grin — stem — club — slot

3. plop — twig — skin — span

4. brick — clash — crush — snuck

Blends

Stop

Stop the

Stop the sled

Stop the sled at

Stop the sled at the

Stop the sled at the flag.

Blends

The

The clock

The clock fell

The clock fell in

The clock fell in the

The clock fell in the crib.

Blends

I

I am

I am glad

I am glad I

I am glad I did

I am glad I did not

I am glad I did not spill

I am glad I did not spill **the**

I am glad I did not spill **the** slush.

ACTIVITY
Beginning Blends

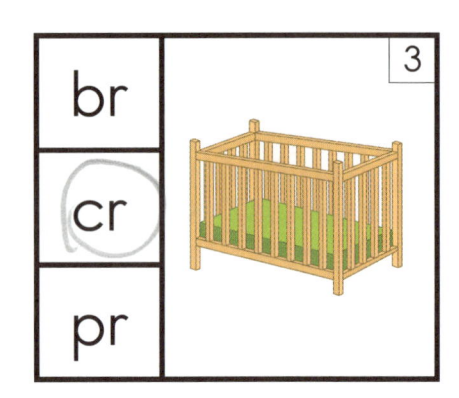

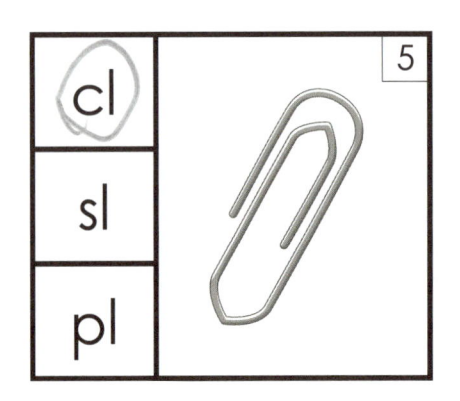

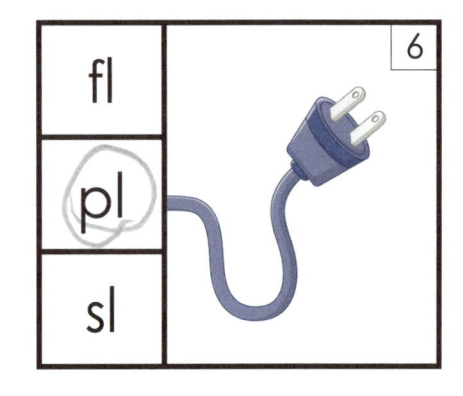

1. Say the name of the picture.
2. Circle the blend that makes the beginning sound of the word.

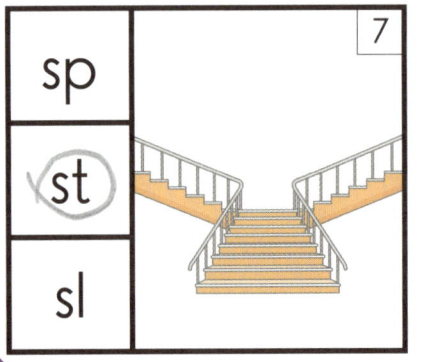

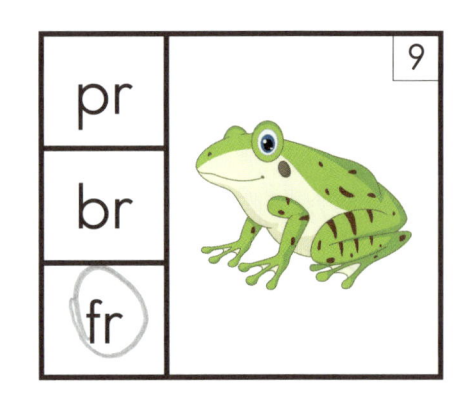

1. fl / (cl) / pl — clock	2. sn / sm / (sw) — swim	3. br / (cr) / pr — crib
4. gl / (gr) / pr — grass	5. (cl) / sl / pl — clip	6. fl / (pl) / sl — plug
7. sp / (st) / sl — stairs	8. (sl) / sp / sm — sled	9. pr / br / (fr) — frog

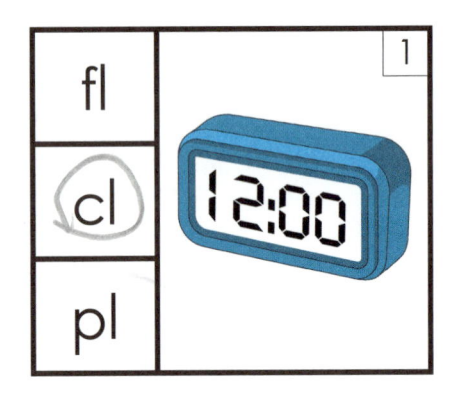

220

ACTIVITY
Beginning Blends / No Blend

1. Look at the picture.
2. Circle the word that matches the picture.

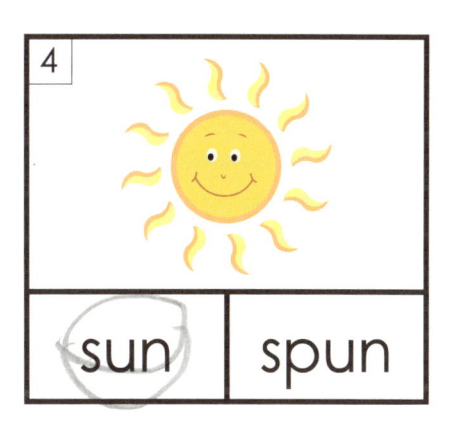

1	cap	(clap)	2	(sip)	snip	3	lock	(block)
4	sun	spun	5	sick	(stick)	6	bush	(brush)
7	(gum)	glum	8	sell	(smell)	9	(pan)	plan

221

ACTIVITY
Beginning Blends

Draw a line from a beginning blend to a word-ending to make words.

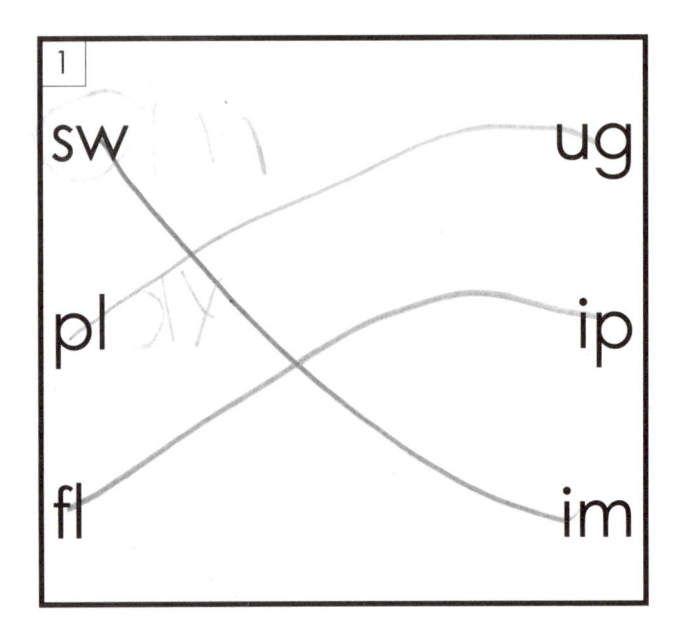

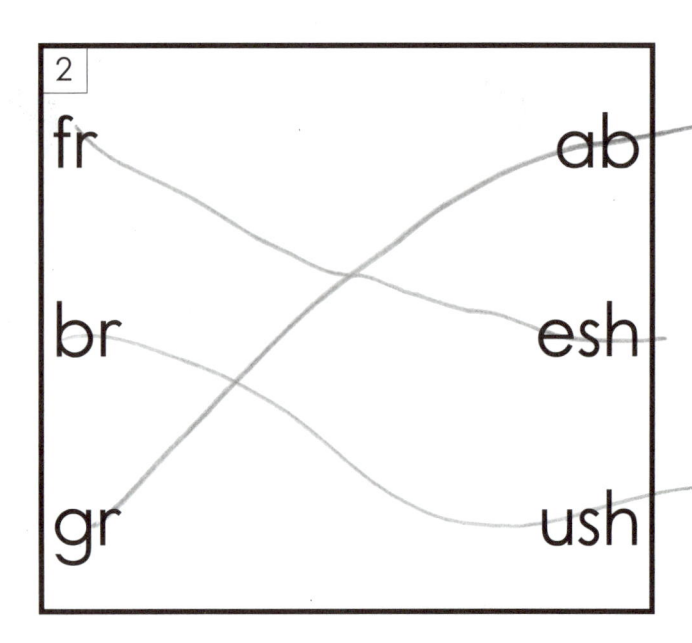

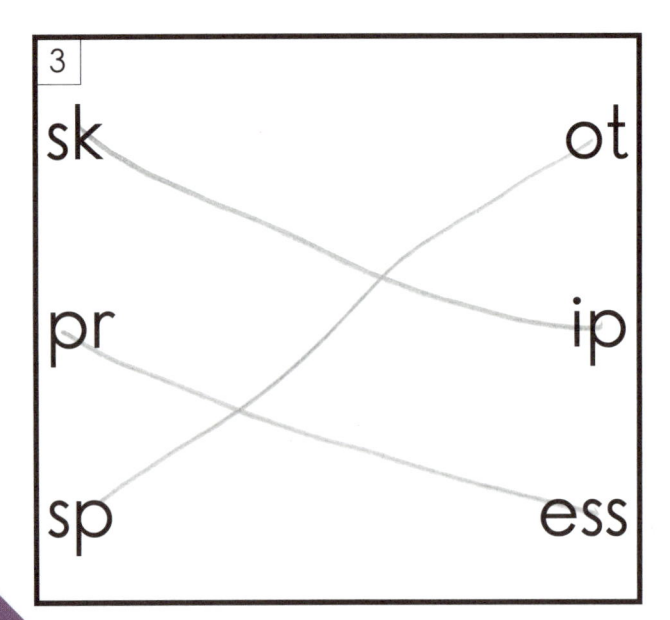

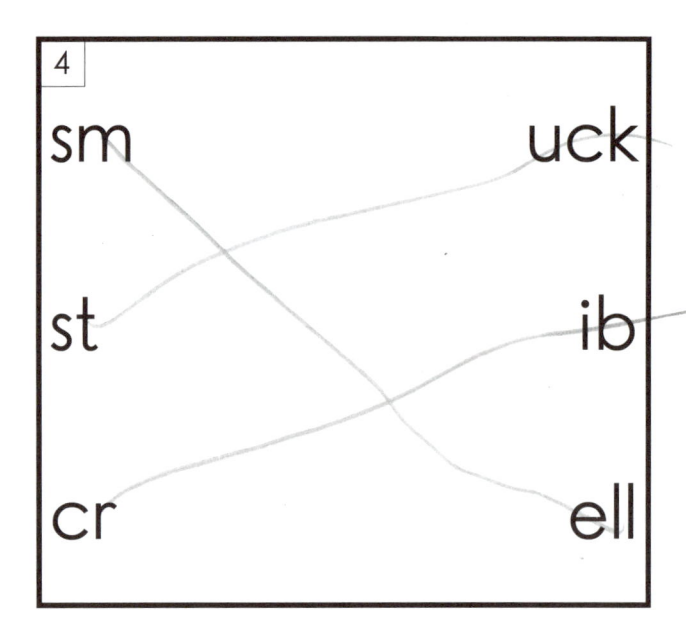

1
sw — im
pl — ug
fl — ip

2
fr — esh
br — ush
gr — ab

3
sk — ess
pr — ot
sp — ip

4
sm — ell
st — uck
cr — ib

222

ACTIVITY
Beginning Blends

1. Read the question.
2. Put a ✓ next to the correct answer.

1 Can a fan clap?	☑ yes	☐ no
2 Can a frog mop?	☐ yes	☑ no
3 Is grass black?	☐ yes	☒ no
4 Can a fish swim?	☑ yes	☐ no
5 Is a brush hot?	☐ yes	☒ no
6 Do you sit on a sled?	☑ yes	☐ no
7 Can you step on a stick?	☑ yes	☐ no

Beginning **drum**

Blends

dr

1. drip   drum   drag

2. drop   drab   drug

3. dress   drill   dram

Note to Teachers: Students should be careful when spelling the /dr/ sound and remember to use **dr** and not **jr**.

READ

224

Beginning

drum

Blends

tr

1. trap — trip — trim

2. trot — track — trod

3. truck — trash — trick

Students should be careful when spelling the /tr/ sound and remember to use **tr** and not **chr**.

Note to Teachers:

READ

Blends

MARK THE WORD

drum

1. Draw a ⌣ under the blend.
2. Say the sound.
3. Read the word.

1. **trip** trap drum drip

2. clap still grid twin

3. sped drop flat brag

4. slim snuff trim skid

WRITE

dr • tr

Drag

Drag **the**

Drag **the** trash

Drag **the** trash **and**

Drag **the** trash **and** drop

Drag **the** trash **and** drop it

Drag **the** trash **and** drop it in

Drag **the** trash **and** drop it in **the**

Drag **the** trash **and** drop it in **the** truck.

ACTIVITY
dr · tr

1. Say the name of the picture.
2. Does the word begin with a **dr** or **tr** sound?
3. Write the answer in the box.

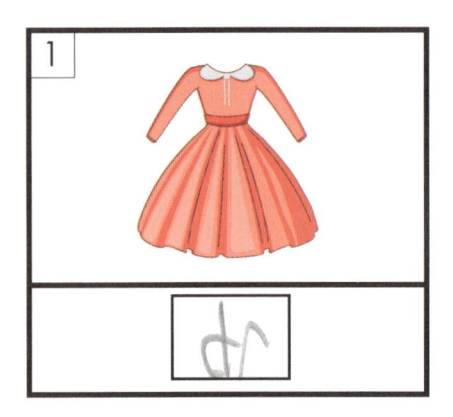

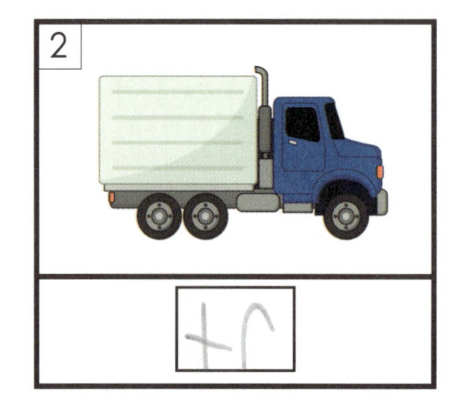

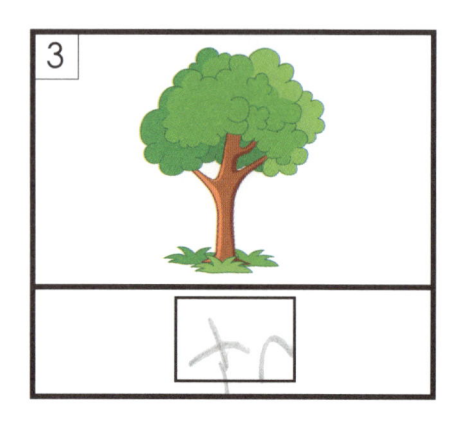

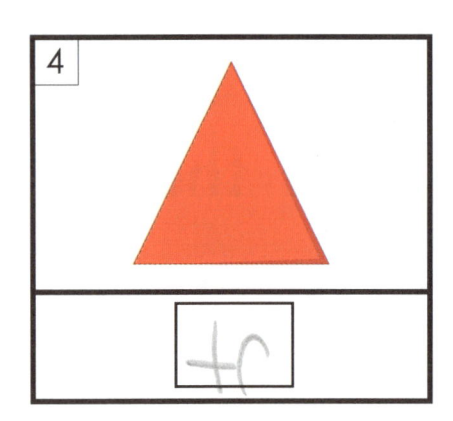

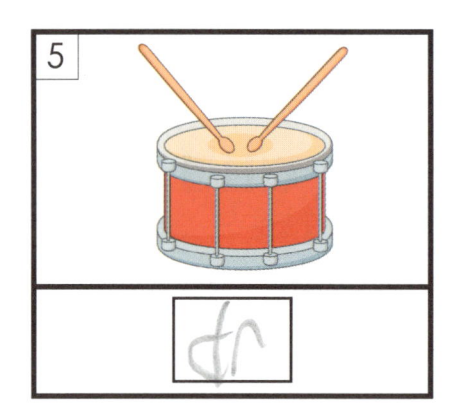

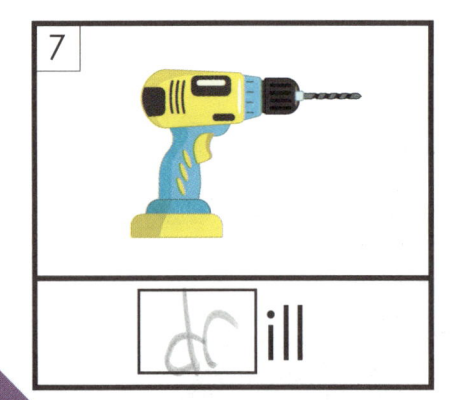

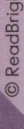

1	2	3
dr	tr	tr

4	5	6
tr	dr	tr

7	8	9
dr ill	tr ash	dr op

228

ACTIVITY
dr · tr

1. Read the question.
2. Put a ✓ next to the correct answer.

1 Can a man trap a bug?	☑ yes	☐ no
2 Can a sled drag a truck?	☐ yes	☒ no
3 Can a drum run and run?	☐ yes	☒ no
4 Can a kid drop a bat?	☑ yes	☐ no
5 Can a doll do a trick?	☐ yes	☒ no
6 Can a dress get wet?	☑ yes	☐ no
7 Can a kid trip on a dish?	☑ yes	☐ no

Phonics Skill: Beginning Blends

Pop Words: look | were | some

POP WORDS

1. I look for tricks,
2. I look for tricks,
3. I look for tricks,
4. To do with bricks.

5. The blocks were tall,
6. The blocks were tall,
7. The blocks were tall,
8. And did not fall.

9. I grab some pins,
10. I grab some pins,
11. I grab some pins,
12. They flip and spin.

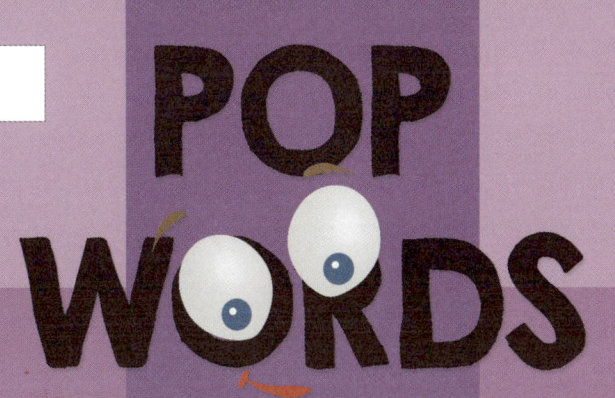

Pop Words: | look | were | some |

POP WORDS

1. were — some — look
2. what — or — when
3. some — which — were
4. how — my — from
5. look — see — your

Pop Words: | look | were | some

POP WORDS

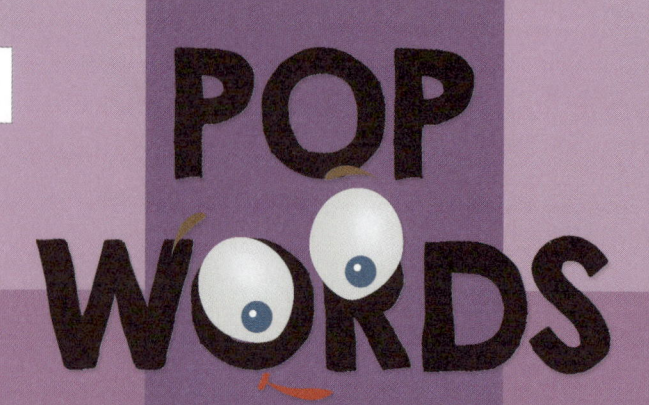

1. Read the pop word in the shaded box.
2. Circle the same pop word in the row next to it.

1 were	was	*were*	we	what
2 look	off	*look*	all	from
3 some	said	*some*	she	was

Unscramble the pop word.
Use the word box if you need a hint.

1 e, r, w, e	were
2 o, k, o, l	look
3 s, m, e, o	some

Word Box

look   some

were

Blends

1. sand   lift   melt
2. pump   gasp   fast
3. dusk   help   went
4. held   rust   milk
5. next   camp   lend

Blends

1. send   raft   hunt

2. dump   test   fact

3. belt   mask   silk

4. ranch   punch   bunch

5. pinch   bench   lunch

Blends

MARK THE WORD

band

1. Draw a ⌣ under the blend.
2. Say the sound.
3. Read the word.

1. felt   bump   rent   land

2. sulk   just   risk   best

3. damp   kept   past   lisp

4. mint   desk   mend   left

Blends

MARK THE WORD

ba**nd**

1. Draw a ︵ under the blend.
2. Say the sound.
3. Read the word.

1. **self**   hand   ramp   last

2. gulp   hint   sift   must

3. sent   dust   tact   bulk

4. bent   task   wept   rest

WRITE

Blends

Dump

Dump sand

Dump sand **on**

Dump sand **on the**

Dump sand **on the** desk.

Blends

I

I can

I can jump

I can jump **and**

I can jump **and** skip

I can jump **and** skip with

I can jump **and** skip with **a**

I can jump **and** skip with **a** glass

I can jump **and** skip with **a** glass **of**

I can jump **and** skip with **a** glass **of** milk.

ACTIVITY
End Blunds

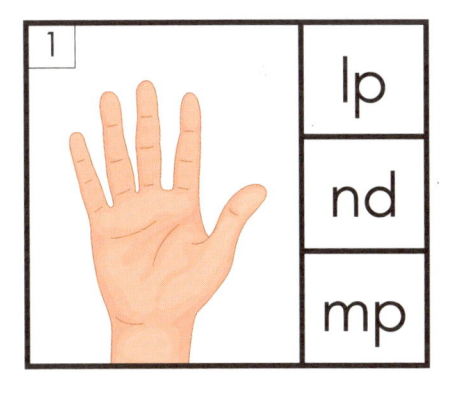

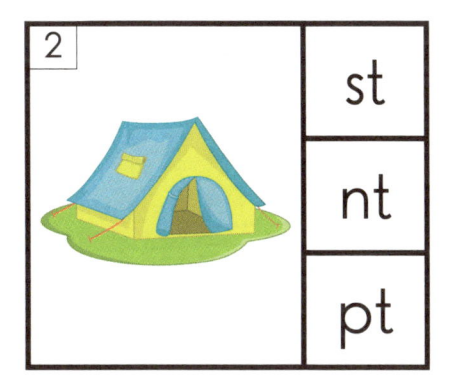

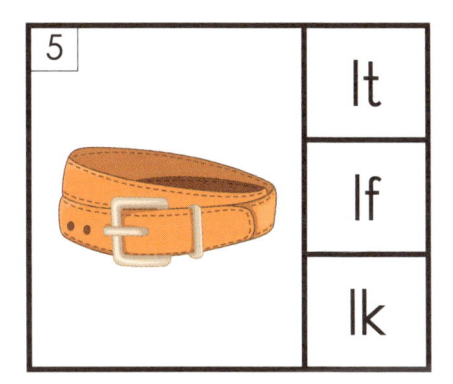

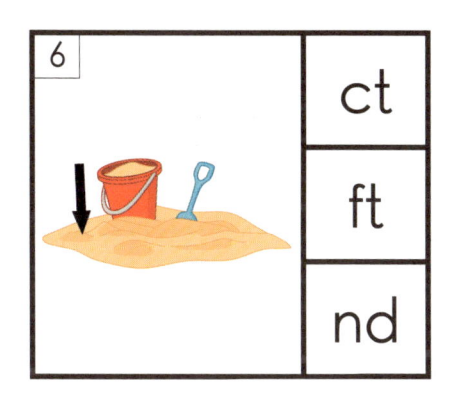

1. Say the name of the picture.
2. Circle the blend that makes the ending sound of the word.

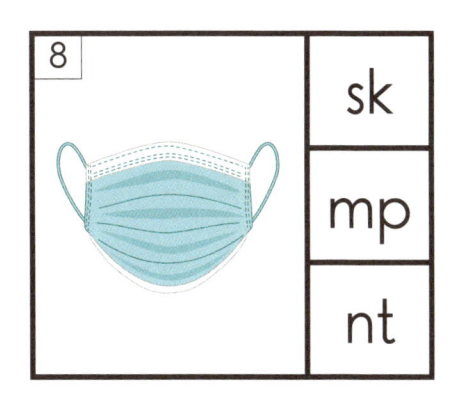

#	Picture	Options
1	hand	lp / nd / mp
2	tent	st / nt / pt
3	skip	mp / nt / st
4	desk	st / sp / sk
5	belt	lt / lf / lk
6	sand	ct / ft / nd
7	milk	ld / lk / nd
8	mask	sk / mp / nt
9	vest	nd / st / sk

239

ACTIVITY
End Blends / No Blend

1. Look at the picture.
2. Circle the word that matches the picture.

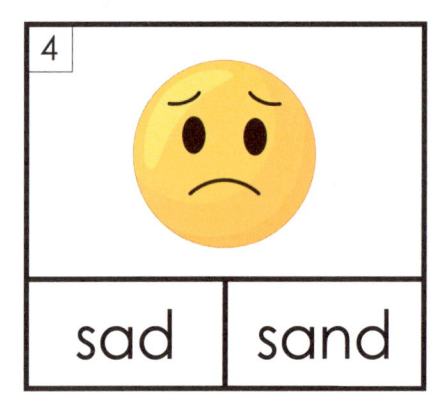

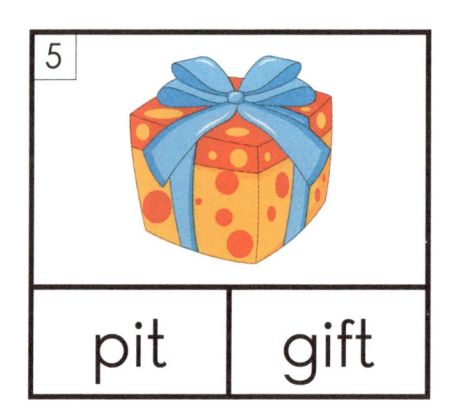

#		
1	met / melt	
2	sit / sift	
3	cat / cast	
4	sad / sand	
5	pit / gift	
6	hum / hump	
7	bed / bend	
8	lap / lamp	
9	net / nest	

ACTIVITY
End Blends

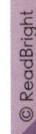

Draw a line from letters on the left side of the box to an end blend to make words.

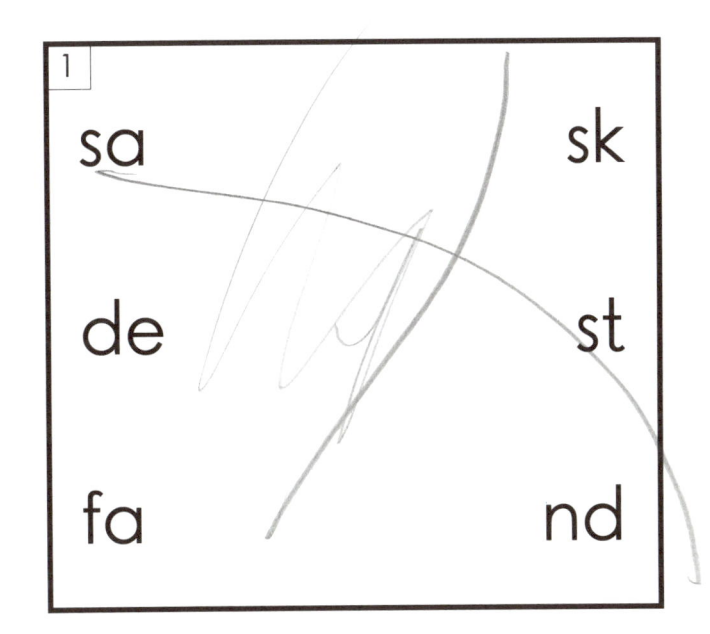

1

sa	sk
de	st
fa	nd

2

se	mp
pu	nd
pa	st

3

se	st
he	nt
ju	lp

4

mi	mp
ca	lt
be	lk

ACTIVITY
End Blends

1. Read the question.
2. Put a ✓ next to the correct answer.

1	Can you rest on a bed?	☐ yes	☐ no
2	Do you jump in camp?	☐ yes	☐ no
3	Can a belt run fast?	☐ yes	☐ no
4	Can a kid help his mom?	☐ yes	☐ no
5	Can a man lift a mask?	☐ yes	☐ no
6	Is it fun to sit in the sand?	☐ yes	☐ no
7	Can milk dust a shelf?	☐ yes	☐ no

Blends

Beginning — drum
End — band

1. blend   grant   clasp
2. trend   crisp   flask
3. slump   plant   stand
4. spent   swept   cramp
5. gland   blast   drift

Blends

1. blunt   grand   clump

2. trust   crest   scant

3. frisk   spend   stunt

4. brand   draft   twist

5. brunch   clench   crunch

Blends

MARK THE WORD

blend

1. Draw a ‿ under the blends in each word.
2. Say the sounds.
3. Read the word.

1. s‿ilt‿   bland   stamp   grasp

2. scalp   crust   clamp   print

3. grunt   plump   stomp   swift

4. spelt   graft   slant   craft

Blends

The

The stick

The stick will

The stick will help

The stick will help the

The stick will help the plant

The stick will help the plant stand

The stick will help the plant stand and

The stick will help the plant stand and not

The stick will help the plant stand and not twist.

ACTIVITY
Beginning & End Blends

1. Say the name of the picture.
2. Look at the pairs of boxes beside each picture.
3. Shade in the box in each pair that has the letter or letters in the word.
4. Write the word in the empty box at the end of the row.

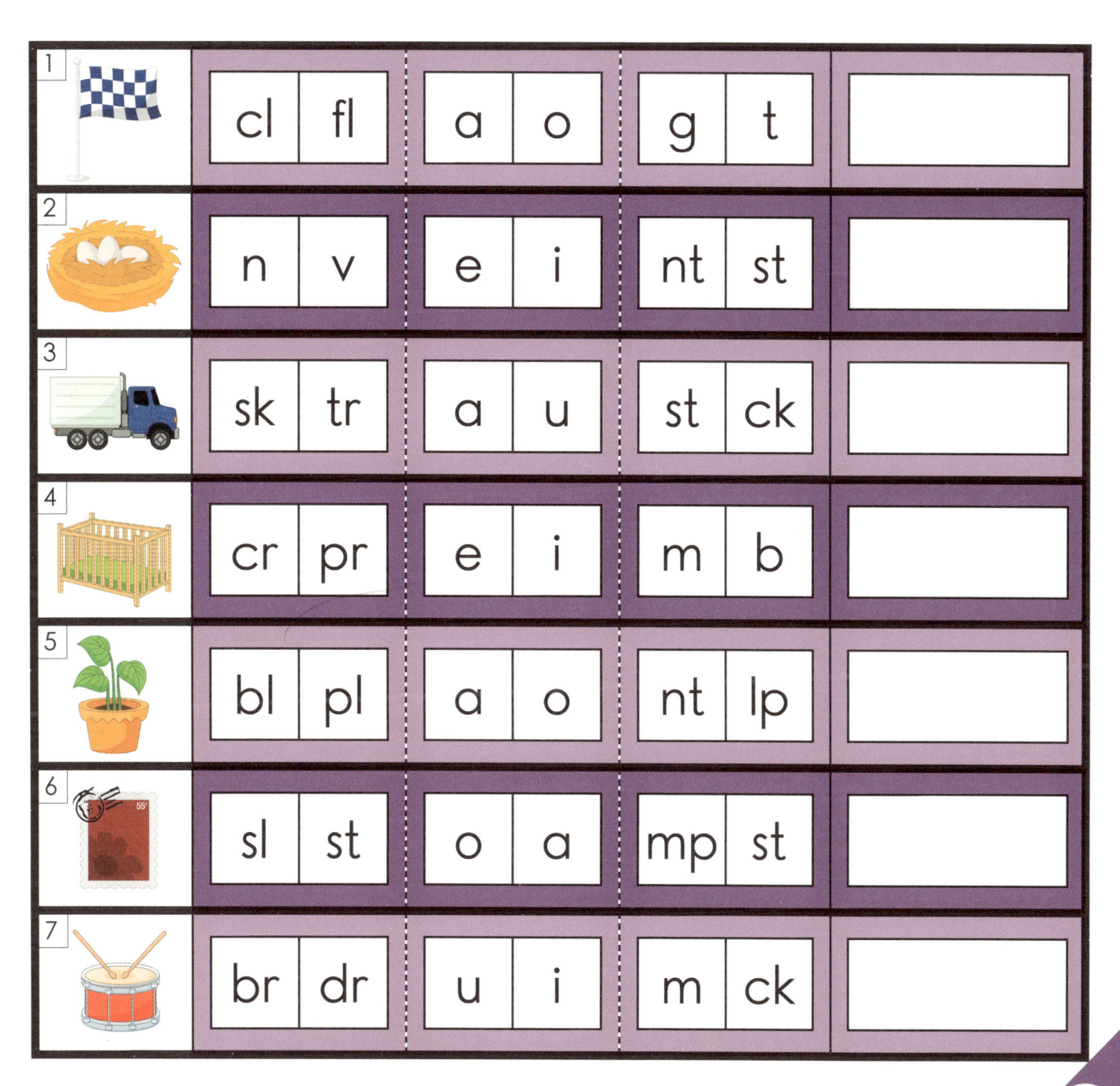

#	Picture	Blend 1	Vowel	Blend 2	Word
1	flag	cl / fl	a / o	g / t	
2	nest	n / v	e / i	nt / st	
3	truck	sk / tr	a / u	st / ck	
4	crib	cr / pr	e / i	m / b	
5	plant	bl / pl	a / o	nt / lp	
6	stamp	sl / st	o / a	mp / st	
7	drum	br / dr	u / i	m / ck	

247

ACTIVITY
Beginning & End Blends

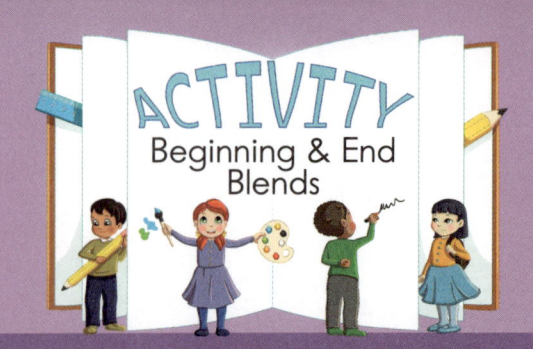

1. Read the sentence.
2. Look at the picture.
3. Circle the ✓ if the picture matches the sentence.
   Circle the ✗ if the picture does not match the sentence.

#	Sentence	Picture	Answer
1	The nest is on the branch.		✓ ✗
2	The milk spills on the stamp.		✓ ✗
3	The duck swam to the plant.		✓ ✗
4	He swept the steps.		✓ ✗
5	The twins stand on the grass.		✓ ✗
6	The bench is next to the stump.		✓ ✗

Beginning Triple-Letter Blends

Blends

1. split   splat   splash

2. splint   scrub   scrap

3. script   strum   strap

4. stress   strip   struck

                       strand

Note to Teachers:
Since triple-letter blends are challenging, you can teach them after you have completed *Sticky Sounds*.

READ

Phonics Skill: End Blends

Pop Words: one 1 two 2 more

POP WORDS

1. I do one jump,
2. I do one jump,
3. I do one jump,
4. And down I bump.

5. I do two hops,
6. I do two hops,
7. I do two hops,
8. And then I flop.

9. I do more bends,
10. I do more bends,
11. I do more bends,
12. And that is the end.

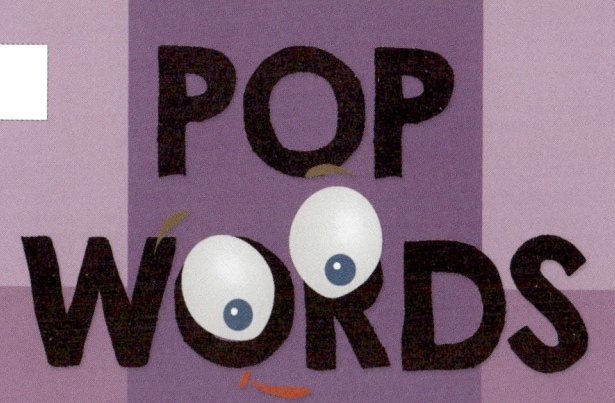

Pop Words: | one | two | more

POP WORDS

1. more   one   two
2. how   some   were
3. see   your   or
4. one   which   look
5. what   more   two

POP WORDS

Pop Words: | one | two | more |

1. Read the pop word in the shaded box.
2. Circle the same pop word in the row next to it.

1	one	on	no	are	one
2	two	this	two	that	how
3	more	some	how	more	with

Unscramble the pop word.
Use the word box if you need a hint.

1	w, t, o	t o w
2	r, e, o, m	__ __ __ __
3	n, o, e	__ __ __

Word Box

one   two

more

STICKY SOUNDS

Sticky Sounds (chunks) refers to a set of frequently paired letters such as *ing*, *ink*, *ung*, *unk*, *ang*, *ank*, *old*, and *ind*.

The *ng* and *nk* combinations are commonly classified as blends. However, the /n/ sound might be neglected because it gets "swallowed up" or stuck to the letter that follows it. Teach students to read *ng* and *nk* combinations as *Sticky Sounds*, rather than blends. By presenting *ng* and *nk* with the preceding vowel, you will help students become aware of the presence of the *n*. This will enhance their spelling and reading accuracy.

ing ank ung
ink ang unk

Sticky Sounds

ing	ink
1. ring king	5. rink wink
2. sing wing	6. link mink
3. thing sting	7. sink pink
4. sling cling	8. blink drink

ing

The

The king

The king has

The king has a

The king has a ring

The king has a ring that

The king has a ring that can

The king has a ring that can sing.

ink

The

The pink

The pink ink

The pink ink is

The pink ink is on

The pink ink is on the

The pink ink is on the sink.

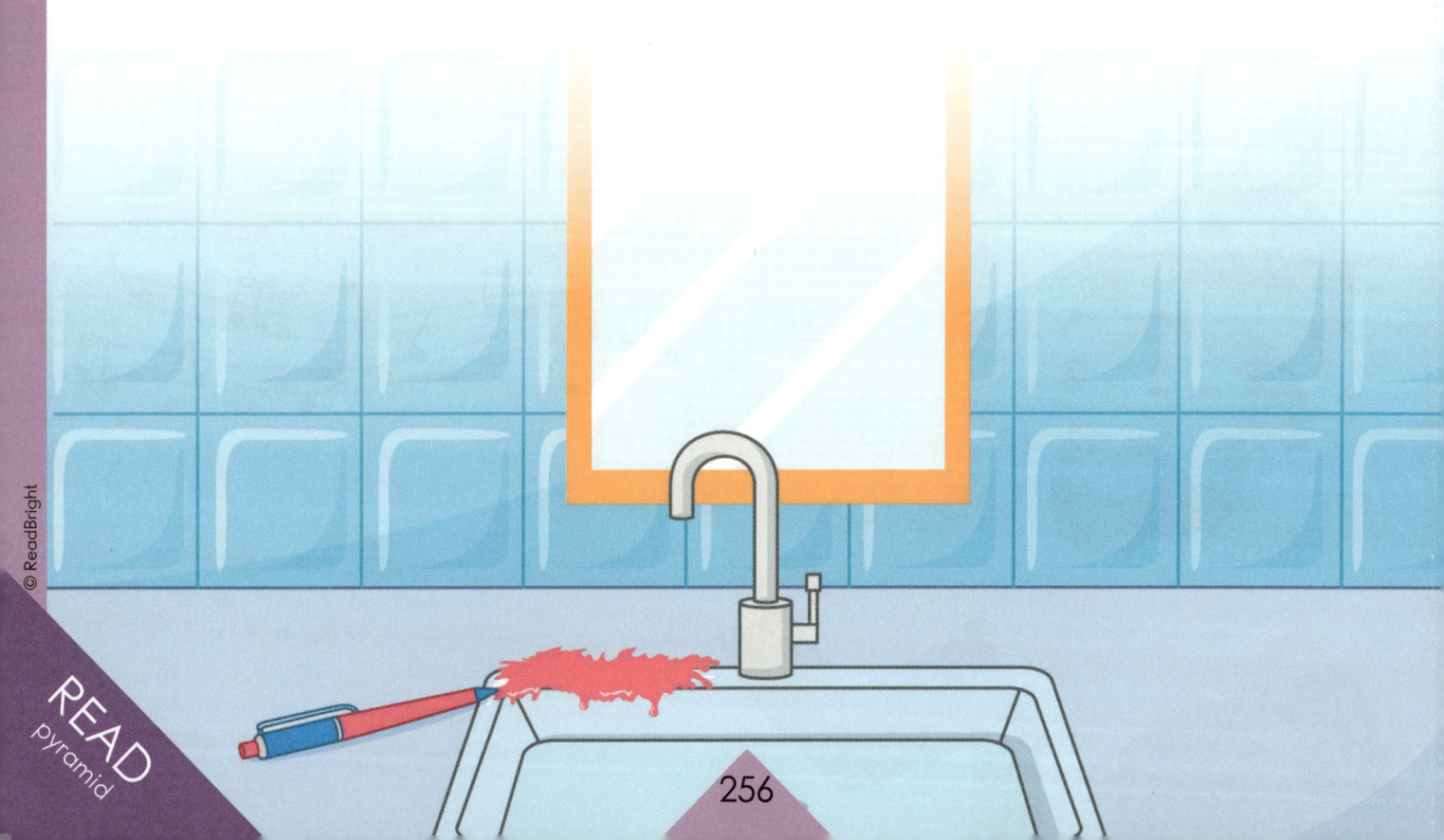

Sticky Sounds

ung	unk
1. sung lung	5. sunk bunk
2. rung hung	6. junk dunk
3. clung stung	7. trunk drunk
4. flung swung	8. flunk spunk

ung

I

I hung

I hung on

I hung on a

I hung on a branch

I hung on a branch and

I hung on a branch and got

I hung on a branch and got stung

I hung on a branch and got stung by

I hung on a branch and got stung by a

I hung on a branch and got stung by a 🐝.

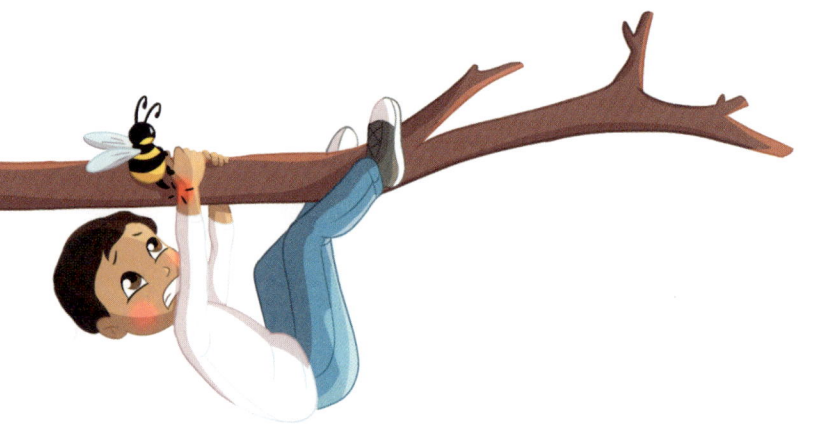

unk

The

The sk<u>unk</u>

The sk<u>unk</u> is

The sk<u>unk</u> is in

The sk<u>unk</u> is in the

The sk<u>unk</u> is in the tr<u>unk</u>.

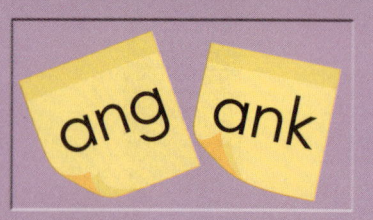

Sticky Sounds

ang	ank
1. sang rang	5. sank tank
2. bang hang	6. blank drank
3. pang tang	7. clank plank
4. slang clang	8. prank crank

ang

The

The bell

The bell r<u>ang</u>

The bell r<u>ang</u> **and**

The bell r<u>ang</u> **and the**

The bell r<u>ang</u> **and the** kids

The bell r<u>ang</u> **and the** kids s<u>ang</u>.

ank

Th**ank**

Th**ank** you

Th**ank** you for

Th**ank** you for the

Th**ank** you for the fish

Th**ank** you for the fish t**ank**.

Sticky Sounds

onk	ong
1. honk	4. song
2. conk	5. long
3. wonk	6. strong

Note to Teachers:

These *Sticky Sounds* are uncommon. Certain English dialects pronounce *ong* as /awng/. Therefore, you can teach it as a *Special Sound* instead.

ong

I

I can

I can sing

I can sing **a**

I can sing **a** long

I can sing **a** long song.

Sticky Sounds

| ing | ink | ung | unk | ang | ank |

1. bang   bank   wing   wink

2. sung   sunk   rang   rank

3. bring   brink   clung   clunk

4. tang   tank   thing   think

Sticky Sounds

MARK THE WORD

ing, ink, ang, ank, ung, unk

1. Circle the *Sticky Sound*.
2. Say the sound.
3. Read the word.

1. k(ing)   ha(ng)   slu(nk)   pi(nk)

2. cla(ng)   lu(ng)   bla(nk)   ti(ng)

3. sa(nk)   bli(nk)   swi(ng)   bu(nk)

4. d(ing)   dra(nk)   flu(ng)   li(nk)

WRITE

ACTIVITY
Sticky Sounds

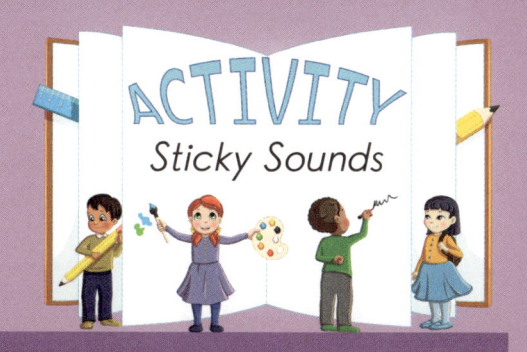

1. Look at the picture.
2. Circle the word that matches the picture.

1	(ring)	rink
2	sing	(sink)
3	sung	(skunk)
4	(bang)	bank
5	(swing)	sing
6	ding	(drink)
7	sunk	(hang)
8	bunk	(bank)
9	(wing)	wink

267

ACTIVITY
Sticky Sounds

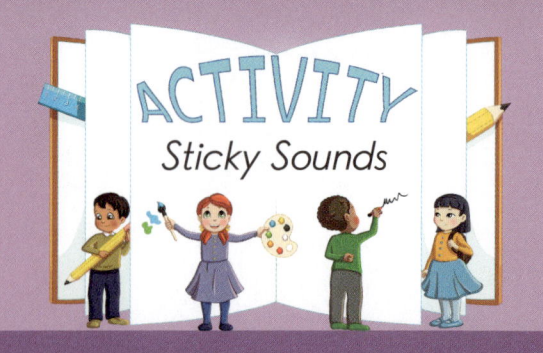

1. Read the question.
2. Put a ✓ next to the correct answer.

1. Did you go to a bank?	☐ yes ☐ no
2. Can you blink and drink?	☐ yes ☐ no
3. Can a ring run?	☐ yes ☐ no
4. Can you sit on a swing?	☐ yes ☐ no
5. Can a kid bang a pot?	☐ yes ☐ no
6. Did you get stung?	☐ yes ☐ no
7. Can a sink sing?	☐ yes ☐ no

POP WORDS

COLORS

- yellow
- orange
- red
- pink
- purple
- blue
- green
- brown
- black
- white

269

POP WORDS

1. Read each word.
2. Color in the circle with a crayon that matches the word.

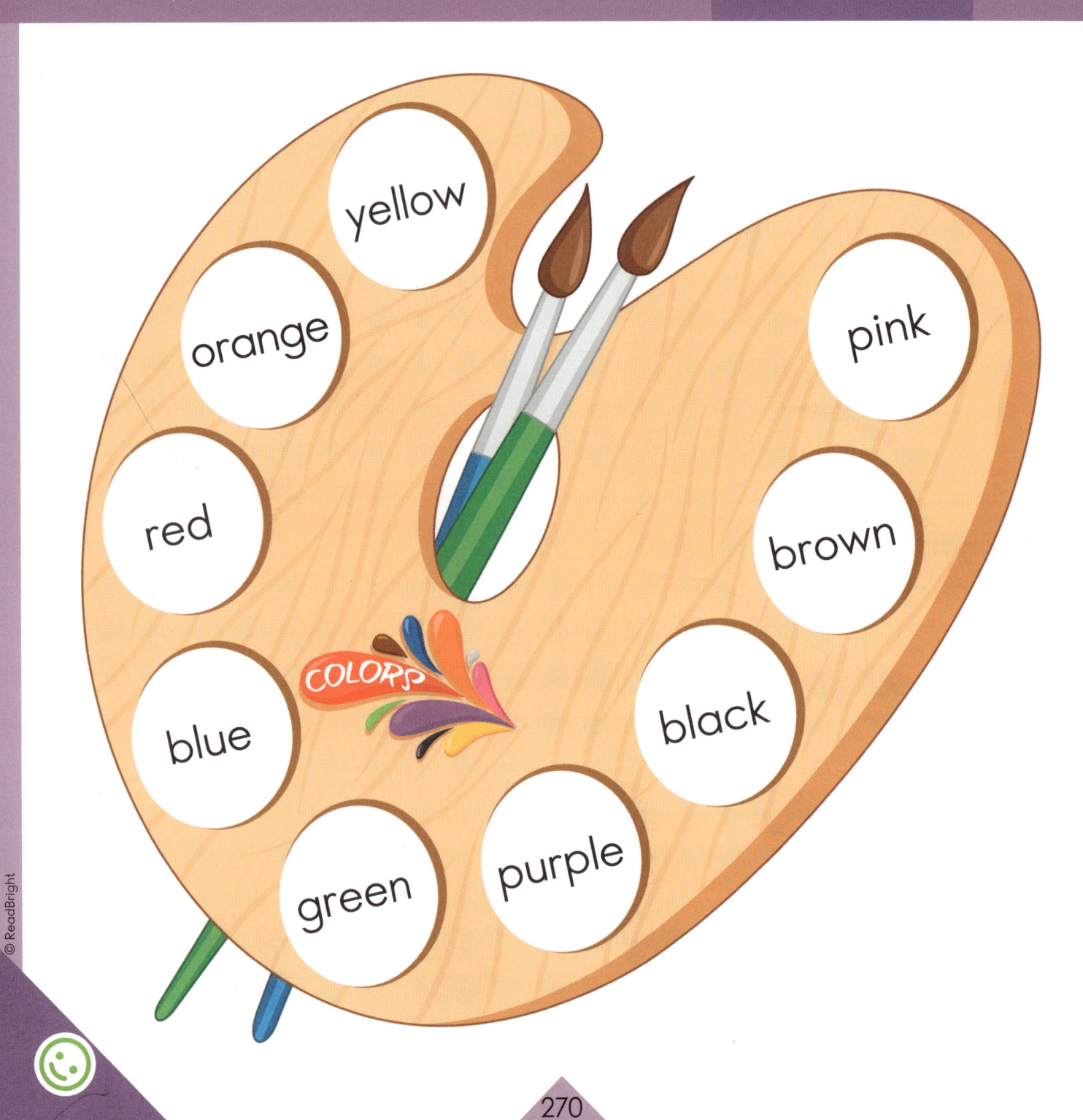

- yellow
- orange
- red
- blue
- green
- pink
- brown
- black
- purple

COLORS

POP WORDS

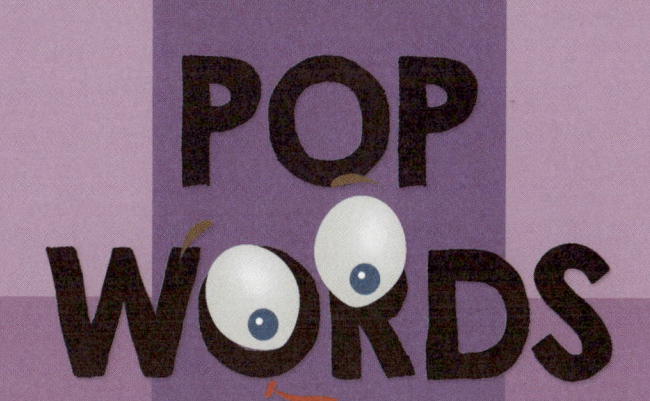

Circle the correct color to finish the sentence.

1	A 🚒 is	purple. / red. / brown.
2	A 🐸 is	red. / pink. / green.
3	A 🚌 is	blue. / green. / yellow.
4	A 🌹 is	black. / pink. / blue.
5	A 🍇 is	purple. / white. / yellow.
6	A ☁️ is	red. / brown. / white.
7	An 🍊 is	blue. / orange. / green.
8	An 🐜 is	black. / orange. / purple.

POP WORDS

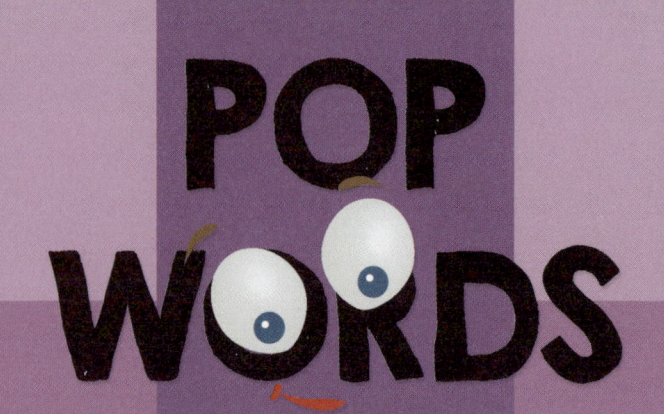

Look at the picture of the clown on the next page.

1. Color the hat **blue**.
2. Color the lips **red**.
3. Color the wig **orange**.
4. Color the hands **yellow**.
5. Color the pants **green**.
6. Color the socks **blue**.
7. Color the 🎀 **pink**.
8. Color the 👀 **brown**.
9. Color the 👐 **purple**.
10. Color the 👞 **black**.
11. Color the balls **yellow** and **red**.

273

POP WORDS

1. color   orange   white
2. black   yellow   green
3. purple   red   blue
4. green   pink   yellow
5. brown   orange   purple

Special Rules

Syllable Division teaches students how to decode words effectively. Students learn that a long word can be divided into smaller, simpler parts. Then, they can read the long word by combining these small pieces together. As an analogy, tell students that a big puzzle is completed by putting small pieces of the puzzle together. Likewise, big words can be read by putting small pieces of the word together.

Special Rules

There are several ways to break a word into syllables:

1. **Words Containing *Twin Letters*:** Divide the word between the *Twin Letters*.
2. **Compound Words:** Break the compound word into two smaller words.
3. **Words Containing Suffixes:** Break the word into the base word and the suffix.

Spelling Rules guides students to achieve proper spelling.

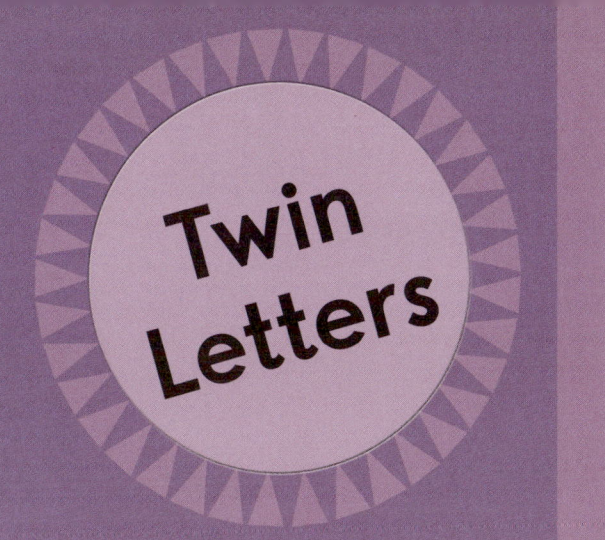

Twin Letters

Syllable Division: When a word contains *Twin Letters*, divide the word between the *Twin Letters*. First read the beginning of the word. Then read the end. Next, read both parts together as one big word.

1. rabbit muffin hiccup

2. summit attic cannot

3. gossip tennis traffic

Twin Letters

The

The ra<u>bb</u>it

The ra<u>bb</u>it has

The ra<u>bb</u>it has a

The ra<u>bb</u>it has a big

The ra<u>bb</u>it has a big mu<u>ff</u>in.

Compound Words

A compound word is a word composed of two real words, such as *bathtub*. Have students look for the two smaller words in a compound word. Once they identify these small words, it will be easy for them to read the words together as a compound word.

1. sun + hat → sunhat
2. cat + nap → catnap
3. sun + tan → suntan
4. bed + bug → bedbug
5. sun + set → sunset

Compound Words

The

The sunhat

The sunhat is

The sunhat is in

The sunhat is in the

The sunhat is in the hatbox.

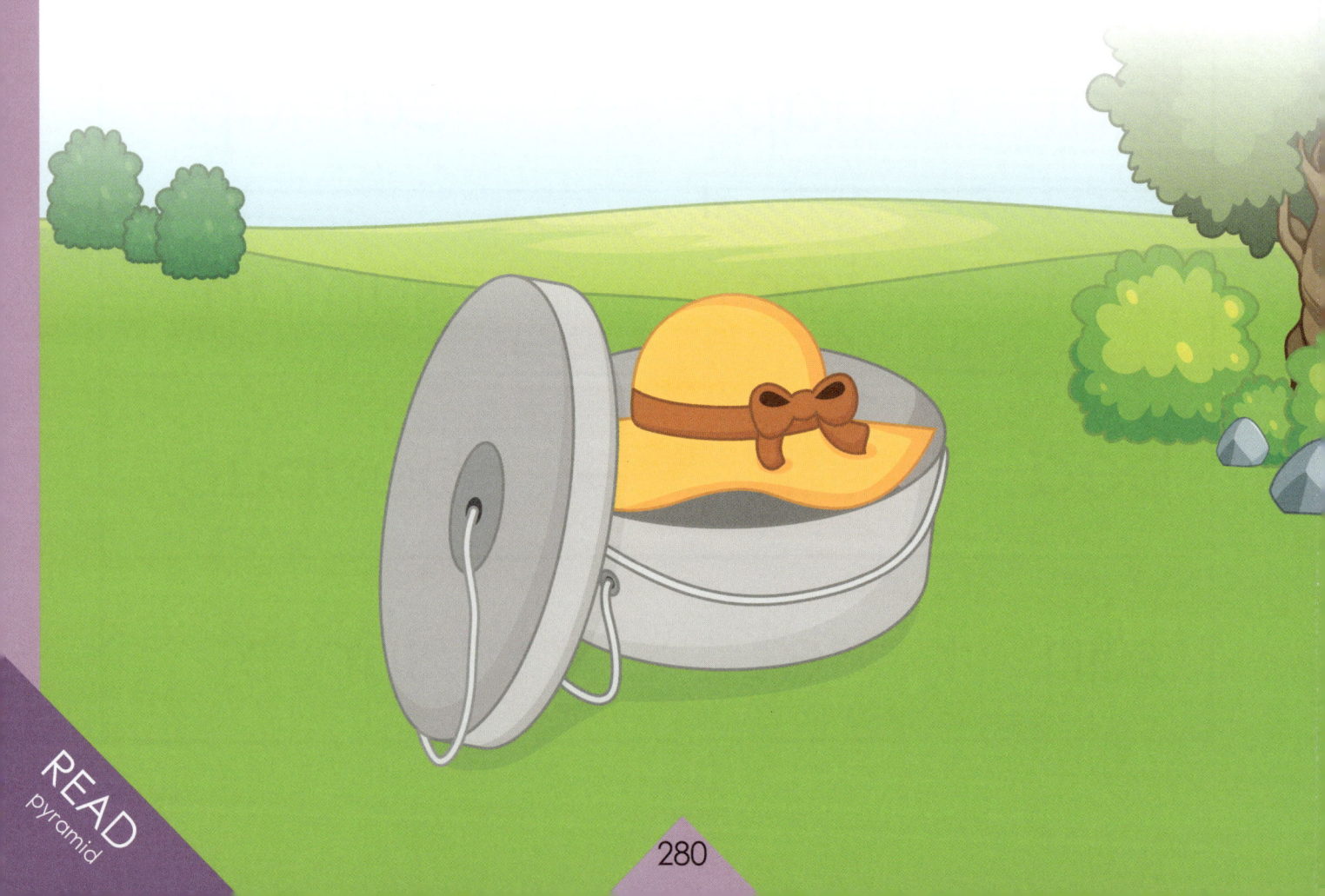

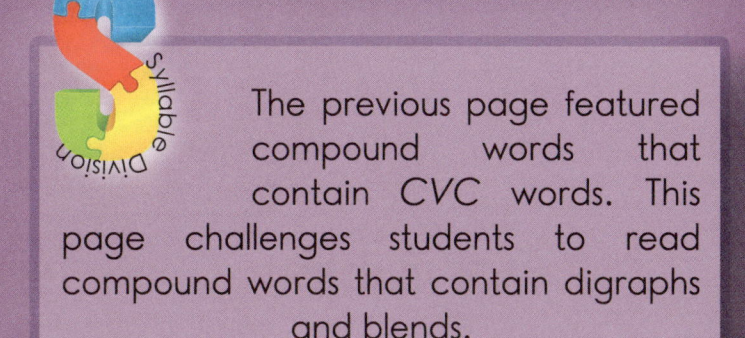

Compound Words

The previous page featured compound words that contain CVC words. This page challenges students to read compound words that contain digraphs and blends.

bath + tub → bathtub

1. gumdrop himself nutshell

2. handheld anthill kickball

3. backdrop itself fishpond

4. lunchbox windmill sunblock

Twin Letters, Compound Words

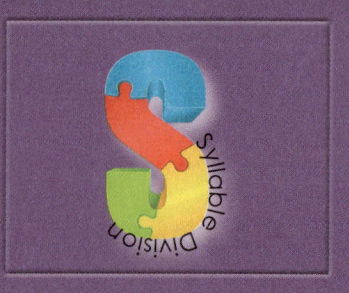

MARK THE WORD

rab|bit

1. a: Draw a line between the *Twin Letters*.
   b: Draw a line between the two small words.
2. Read each word part.
3. Read the whole word.

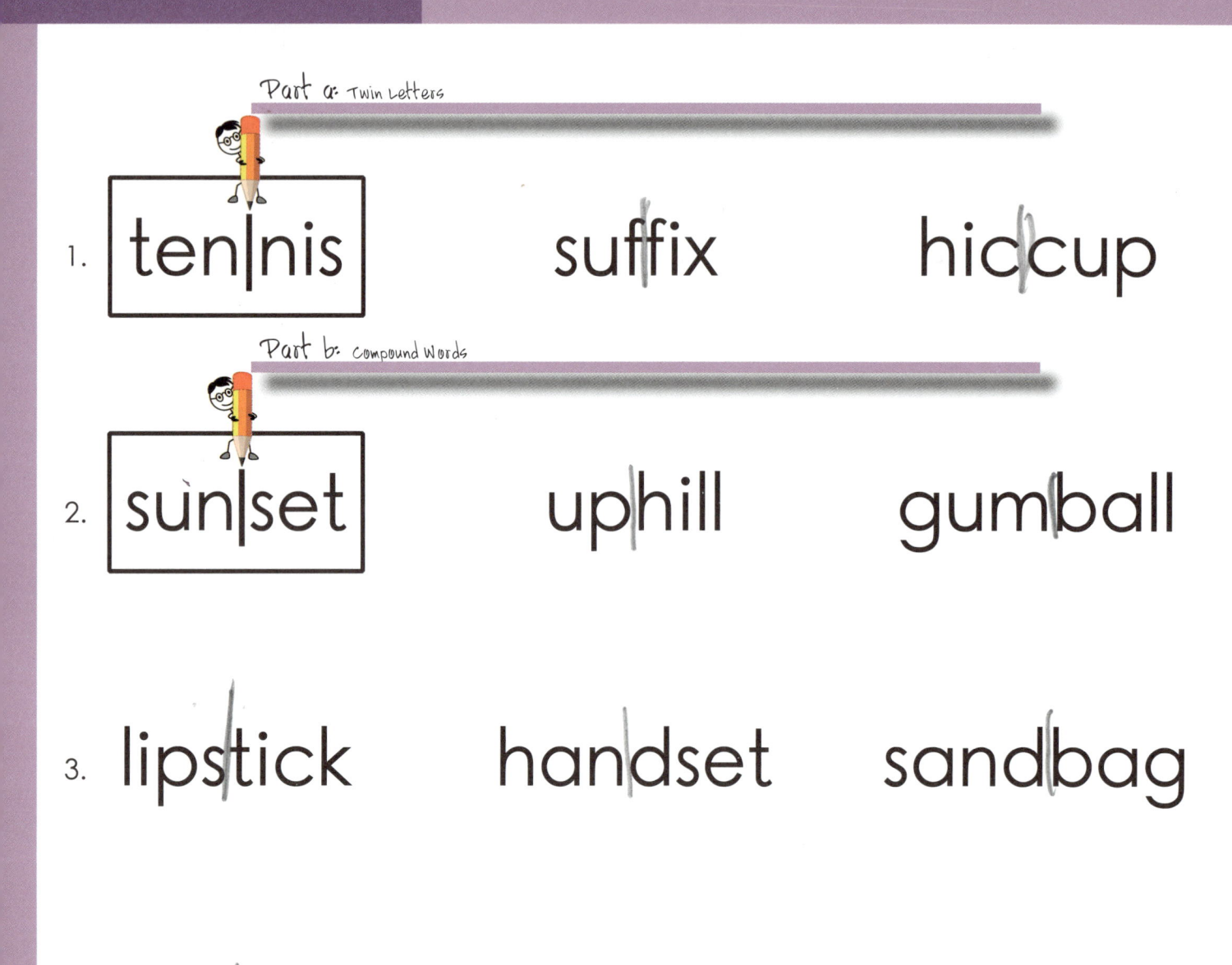

Part a: Twin Letters

1. ten|nis   suf|fix   hic|cup

Part b: Compound Words

2. sun|set   up|hill   gum|ball

3. lip|stick   hand|set   sand|bag

4. cat|fish   milk|man   hand|bag

Compound Words

The

The backpack

The backpack is

The backpack is in

The backpack is in the

The backpack is in the sandbox.

ACTIVITY
Compound Words

1. Say both words to create a compound word.
2. Write the new word on the line.

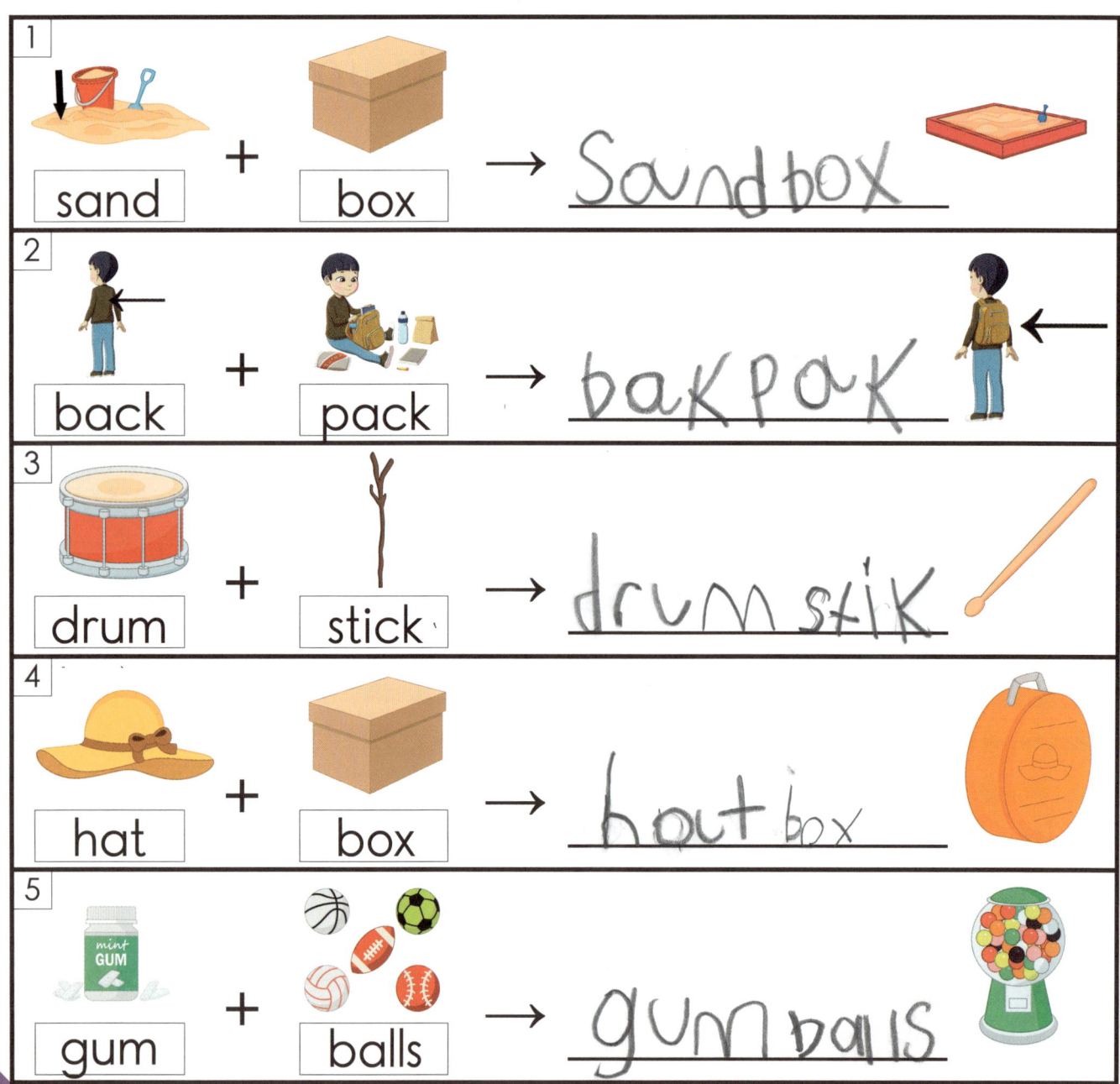

1	sand	+ box	→ Sandbox
2	back	+ pack	→ bakpak
3	drum	+ stick	→ drumstik
4	hat	+ box	→ hautbox
5	gum	+ balls	→ gumballs

ACTIVITY
Compound Words

Draw a line from a word in the first column to a word in the second column to create a compound word.

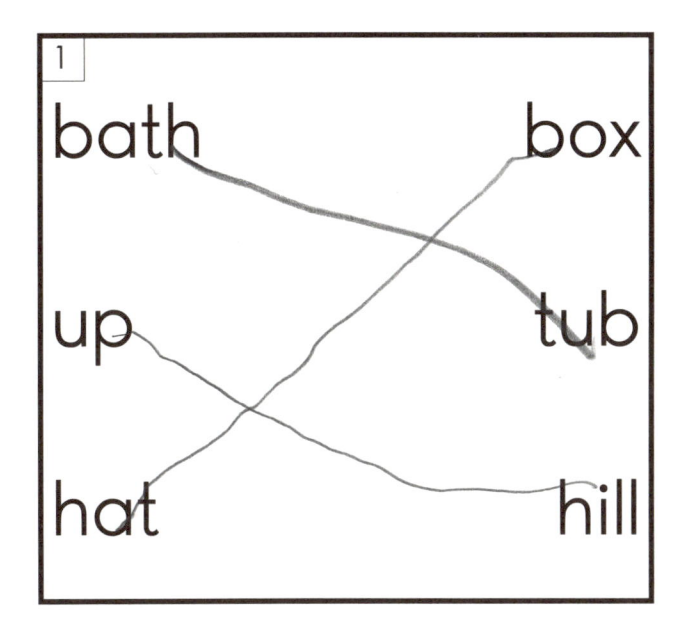

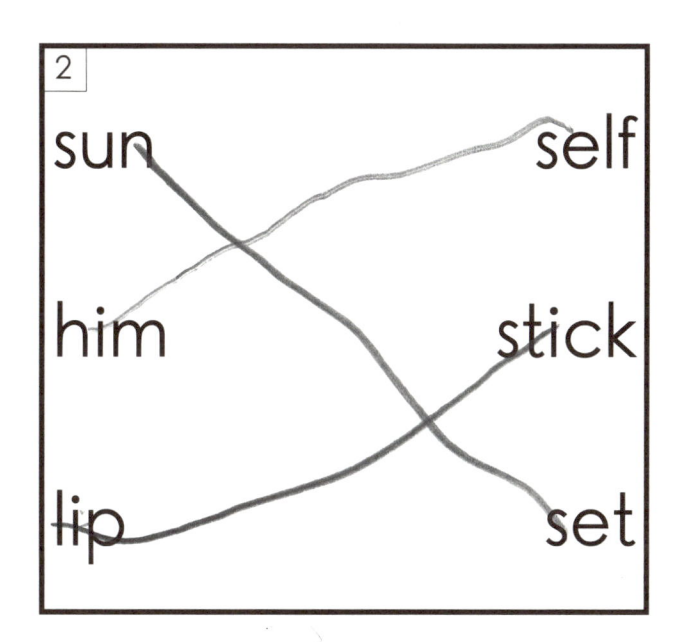

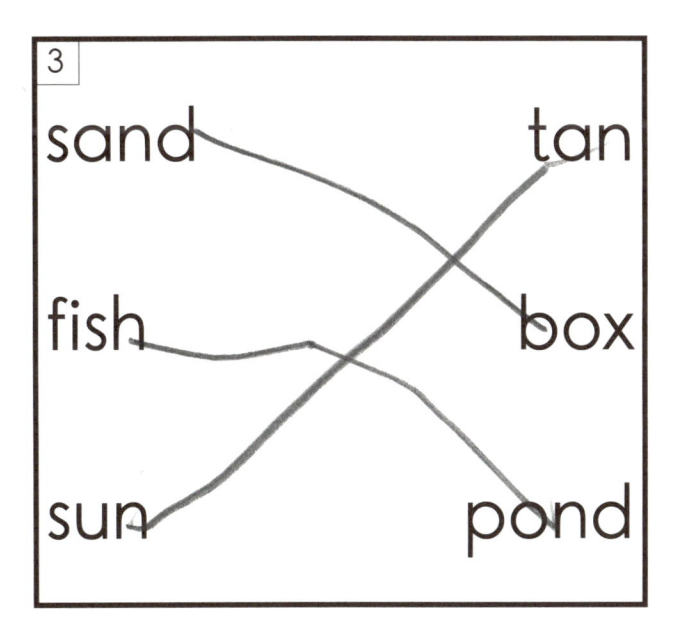

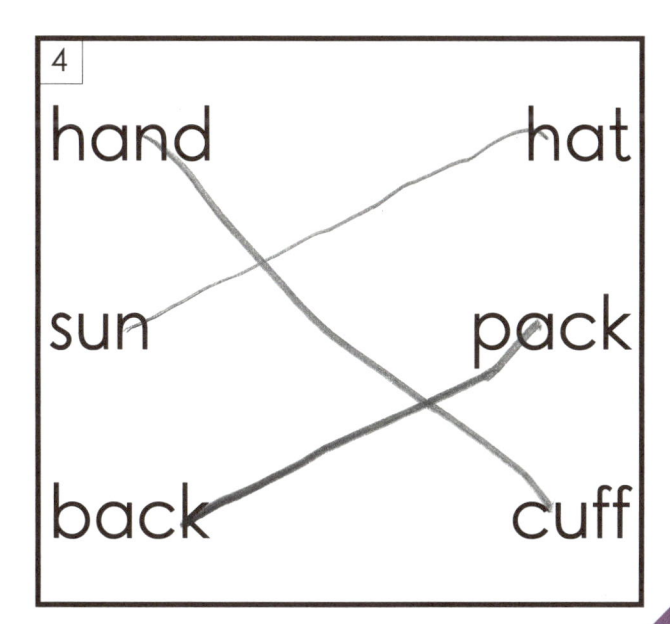

1

bath — tub
up — hill
hat — box

2

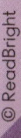

sun — set
him — self
lip — stick

3

sand — box
fish — pond
sun — tan

4

hand — cuff
sun — hat
back — pack

285

Phonics Skill: Compound Words

Pop Words: like out into

POP WORDS

1. I like to snack,
2. I like to snack,
3. I like to snack,
4. From my backpack.

5. Out from the top,
6. Out from the top,
7. Out from the top,
8. Falls a gumdrop.

9. Into my hands,
10. Into my hands,
11. Into my hands,
12. A gumdrop lands.

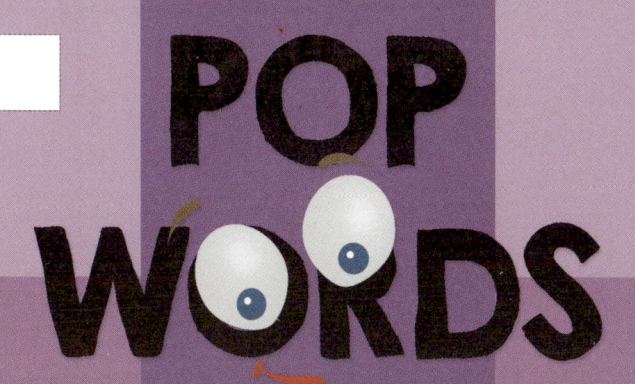

Pop Words: | like | out | into |

POP WORDS

1. out — like — into
2. see — were — one
3. more — into — how
4. two — some — look
5. like — out — your

Pop Words: | like | out | into

POP WORDS

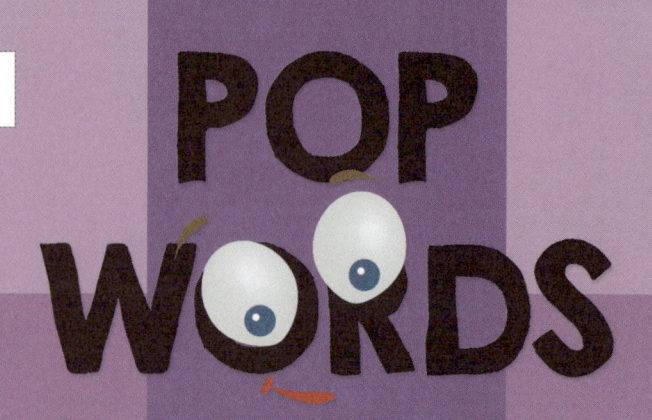

1. Read the pop word in the shaded box.
2. Circle the same pop word in the row next to it.

#					
1	out	or	you	out	that
2	into	in	into	to	one
3	like	look	into	this	like

Unscramble the pop word.
Use the word box if you need a hint.

#		
1	t, u, o	__ __ __
2	t, n, i, o	__ __ __ __
3	e, k, l, i	__ __ __ __

Word Box

like   out

into

Suffix ing

A suffix *ing* indicates that a verb is in the present tense.

To read words containing the suffix *ing*:
- Cover the suffix *ing* with your thumb.
- Read the base word.
- Lift your thumb.
- Read the whole word.

1. rocking   dusting   helping
2. lending   fishing   licking
3. hunting   rushing   sending
4. smelling   thinking   pressing
5. planting   pinching   stamping

Suffix ing

MARK THE WORD

ing

1. Circle the suffix *ing*.
2. Read the base word.
3. Read the suffix.
4. Read the whole word.

1. lift(ing)   wish(ing)   pick(ing)

2. land(ing)   dump(ing)   sift(ing)

3. hint(ing)   spend(ing)   last(ing)

4. test(ing)   stand(ing)   wink(ing)

WRITE

Suffix *ing*

I

I am

I am flipp<u>ing</u>,

I am flipp<u>ing</u>, kick<u>ing</u>,

I am flipp<u>ing</u>, kick<u>ing</u>, **and**

I am flipp<u>ing</u>, kick<u>ing</u>, **and** swimm<u>ing</u>.

ACTIVITY
Suffix *ing*

1. Read the word.
2. Write the suffix ing in the box.
3. Write the new word on the line.
4. Read the new word.

1	suck ☐	_____
2	rent ☐	_____
3	drink ☐	_____
4	hang ☐	_____
5	camp ☐	_____
6	hand ☐	_____
7	bump ☐	_____

Suffix ing

Spelling Rules: When adding the suffix *ing* to a word, double the last letter of the base word if the base word:
- is a CVC word, such as *win*.
- ends in a CVC pattern, such as s*top*.

1. hop + ing → hopping
2. get + ing → getting
3. win + ing → winning
4. slip + ing → slipping
5. stop + ing → stopping
6. plug + ing → plugging

ACTIVITY
Suffix *ing* Spelling Rule

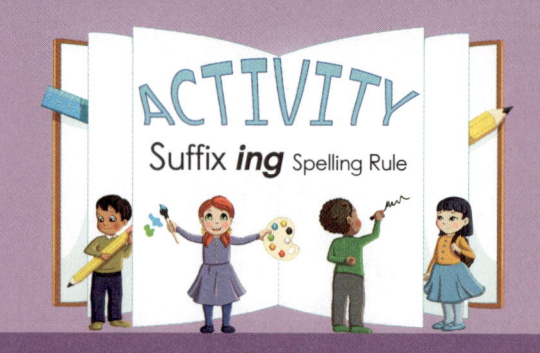

1. Read the word.
2. Write the letter that gets doubled on the line.
3. Write the suffix **ing** in the box.
4. Write the new word on the next line. Then read it.

1	let _t_ [ing]	letting
2	dig _g_ [ing]	digging
3	rub _b_ [ing]	rubing
4	trip _p_ [ing]	triping
5	skip _p_ [ing]	skiping
6	drop _p_ [ing]	droping
7	spin _n_ [ing]	spining

ACTIVITY
Suffix ing Spelling Rule

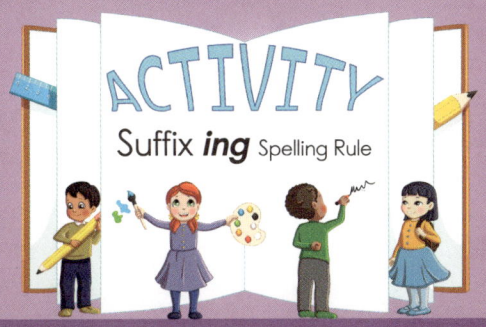

1. Read the word. Is a double letter needed before you add **ing**?
   - If **yes**, write the letter you need to double on the line.
   - If **no**, make a **/** through the line.
2. Write the new word on the next line. Then read it.

#	Word	New Word
1	think ___ ing	_____
2	sip ___ ing	_____
3	swim ___ ing	_____
4	fish ___ ing	_____
5	hop ___ ing	_____

Phonics Skill: Suffix *ing*

Pop Words: first | now | come

POP WORDS

1. First we are mopping.
2. First we are mopping.
3. First we are mopping.
4. Mop! No stopping!

5. Now we are brushing.
6. Now we are brushing.
7. Now we are brushing.
8. Brush! No rushing!

9. Come, let's run.
10. Come, let's run.
11. Come, let's run.
12. Scrub! What fun!

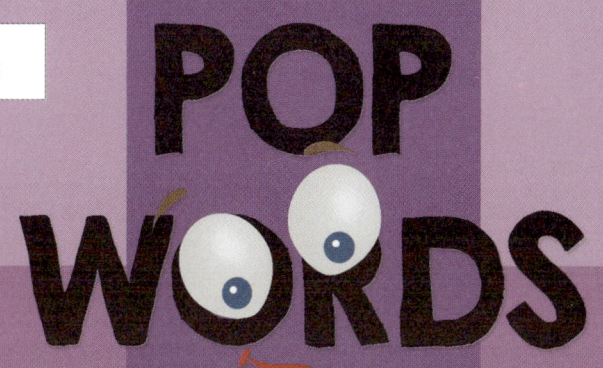

Pop Words: first | now | come

POP WORDS

1. come — now — first
2. into — one — like
3. look — come — were
4. now — two — some
5. more — out — first

Pop Words: | first | now | come |

POP WORDS

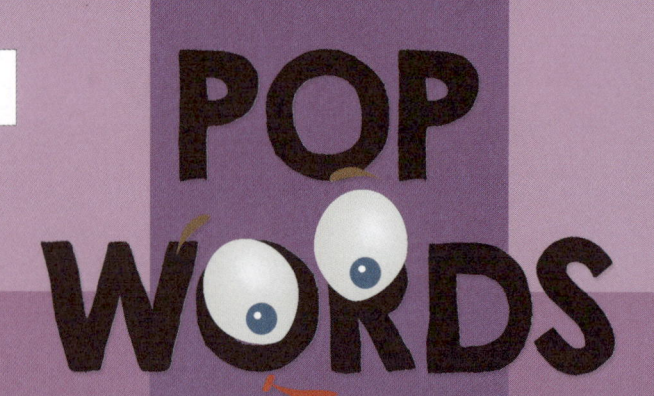

1. Read the pop word in the shaded box.
2. Circle the same pop word in the row next to it.

1 now	how	down	(now)	no
2 come	some	me	more	(come)
3 first	from	off	(first)	this

Unscramble the pop word.
Use the word box if you need a hint.

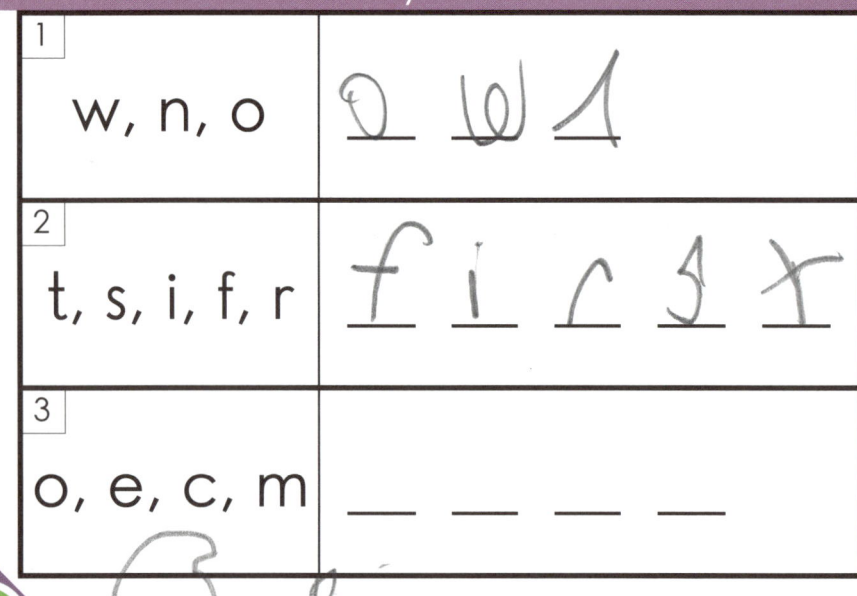

1 w, n, o	___ ___ ___
2 t, s, i, f, r	f i r s t
3 o, e, c, m	___ ___ ___ ___

Word Box

come   now

first

Suffix ed /t/

A suffix *ed* indicates that a verb is in the past tense.

To read words containing the suffix *ed*:
- Cover the suffix *ed* with your thumb.
- Read the base word.
- Lift your thumb.
- Read the whole word.

1. helped   linked   milked
2. dressed   blocked   jumped
3. brushed   picked   tricked
4. pinched   risked   winked
5. grasped   cracked   smashed

Suffix ed /d/

Suffix *ed* can make three different sounds:
1. /t/
2. /d/
3. /ed/

1. filled   called   yelled
2. drilled   smelled   chilled
3. spilled   spelled   stalled
4. willed   swelled   banged
5. milled   shelled   thrilled

Suffix ed /ed/

The /ed/ sound is applied when the base word ends with a /t/ or /d/.

1. tested   busted   hinted
2. shifted   crafted   landed
3. hunted   mended   listed
4. rented   drifted   handed
5. trusted   granted   blended

Suffix ed

Helpful Tip: Here is a way to choose the appropriate sound for the suffix ed: Cover the suffix and pronounce the base word in its past tense. Next, uncover the ed and read the whole word.

1. dusted   yelled   pressed
2. grilled   planted   punched
3. lasted   gulped   smelled
4. drilled   stamped   printed
5. filled   blinked   lifted

Suffix ed

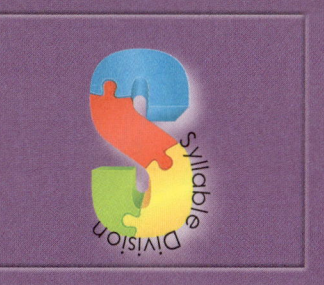

MARK THE WORD

ed

1. Circle the suffix *ed*.
2. Read the base word.
3. Read the whole word.

1. sift(ed) spilled crushed
2. called melted locked
3. rushed landed spelled
4. helped banged rested

Suffix ed /t/

I

I hopp<u>ed</u>,

I hopp<u>ed</u>, skipp<u>ed</u>,

I hopp<u>ed</u>, skipp<u>ed</u>, **and**

I hopp<u>ed</u>, skipp<u>ed</u>, **and** jump<u>ed</u>.

Suffix ed /d/

I

I hugg<u>ed</u>

I hugg<u>ed</u> **the**

I hugg<u>ed</u> **the** doll

I hugg<u>ed</u> **the** doll **and**

I hugg<u>ed</u> **the** doll **and** grinn<u>ed</u>.

Suffix ed /ed/

The

The bug

The bug land<u>ed</u>

The bug land<u>ed</u> on

The bug land<u>ed</u> on the

The bug land<u>ed</u> on the grass

The bug land<u>ed</u> on the grass we

The bug land<u>ed</u> on the grass we plant<u>ed</u>.

ACTIVITY: Suffix *ed*

1. Read the word.
2. Write the suffix ed in the box.
3. Write the new word on the line.
4. Read the new word.

#	Word	New word
1	list ☐	_____
2	crack ☐	_____
3	grill ☐	_____
4	hand ☐	_____
5	wink ☐	_____
6	yell ☐	_____
7	hint ☐	_____

ACTIVITY
Suffix *ing*/*ed*

1. Look at the picture.
2. If it shows something happening now, write `ing` in the box.
   If it shows something that already happened, write `ed` in the box.

1	rest ☐	rest ☐
2	kick ☐	kick ☐
3	snack ☐	snack ☐
4	fill ☐	fill ☐
5	brush ☐	brush ☐
6	melt ☐	melt ☐

308

Suffix ed

Spelling Rules: When adding the suffix *ed* to a word, double the last letter of the base word if the base word:
- is a CVC word, such as *hum*.
- ends in a CVC pattern, such as *clap*.

1. nap + ed → napped
2. pat + ed → patted
3. hum + ed → hummed
4. clap + ed → clapped
5. drag + ed → dragged
6. spot + ed → spotted

ACTIVITY
Suffix **ed** Spelling Rule

1. Read the word.
2. Write the letter that gets doubled on the line.
3. Write the suffix `ed` in the box.
4. Write the new word on the next line. Then read it.

1	tap ___ ☐	_____
2	pin ___ ☐	_____
3	dot ___ ☐	_____
4	drop ___ ☐	_____
5	grab ___ ☐	_____
6	rot ___ ☐	_____
7	step ___ ☐	_____

ACTIVITY
Suffix **ed** Spelling Rule

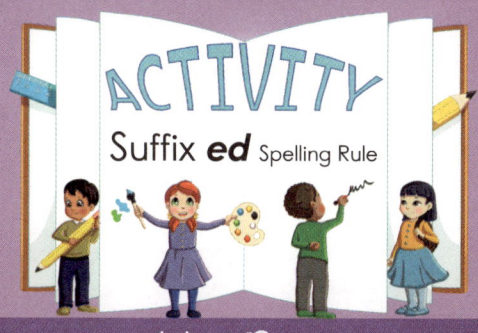

1. Read the word. Is a double letter needed before you add **ed**?
   - If **yes**, write the letter you need to double on the line.
   - If **no**, make a **/** through the line.
2. Write the new word on the next line. Then read it.

#		Word	New Word
1		lock ___ ed	_____
2		rip ___ ed	_____
3		slip ___ ed	_____
4		pack ___ ed	_____
5		mop ___ ed	_____

Phonics Skill: Suffix *ed*

Pop Words: these   other   many

POP WORDS

1. I filled these sacks,
2. I filled these sacks,
3. I filled these sacks,
4. With blocks and tracks.

5. I helped other kids,
6. I helped other kids,
7. I helped other kids,
8. With pots and lids.

9. I packed many bags,
10. I packed many bags,
11. I packed many bags,
12. With hats and rags.

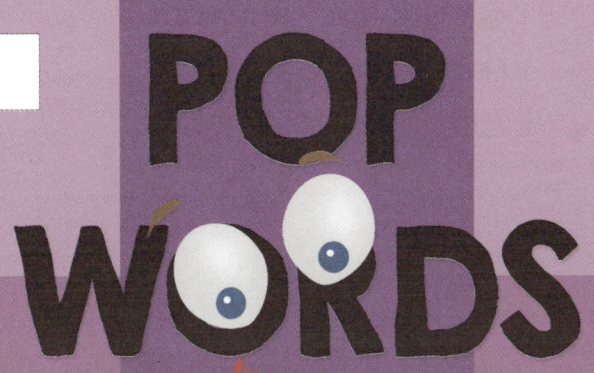

Pop Words: | these | other | many

POP WORDS

1. other — these — many
2. come — into — now
3. out — first — two
4. like — many — more
5. these — one — other

Pop Words: | these | other | many |

POP WORDS

1. Read the pop word in the shaded box.
2. Circle the same pop word in the row next to it.

1 many	more	many	some	come
2 other	the	out	they	other
3 these	this	the	these	then

Unscramble the pop word.
Use the word box if you need a hint.

1 y, m, n, a	_ _ _ _
2 e, e, s, h, t	_ _ _ _ _
3 r, o, h, e, t	_ _ _ _ _

Word Box

other   these

many

314

k or ck?

Spelling Rules

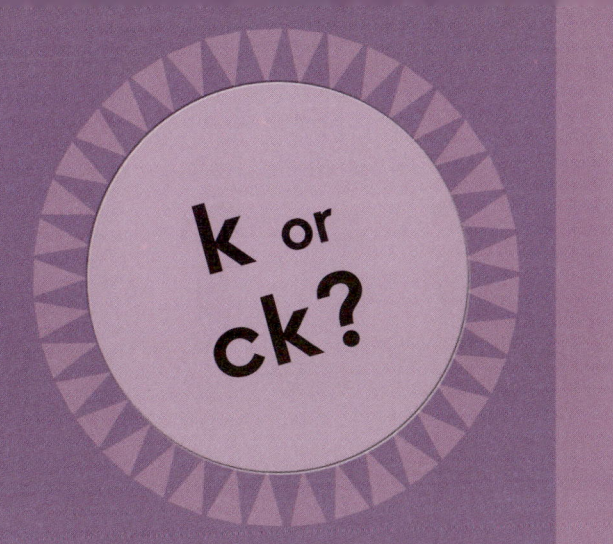

A /k/ sound at the end of a word is spelled **k** or **ck**.
If the first vowel of the word is followed by a consonant or another vowel (a "helper"), write a **k**.
If the first vowel of the word is **not** followed by a consonant or another vowel (a "helper"), write a **ck**.

k	ck
1. silk blank	5. back stick
2. bulk drink	6. neck pluck
3. risk spunk	7. dock black
4. task flask	8. kick snuck

ACTIVITY
k or ck Spelling Rule

1. Look at the picture.
2. Write k or ck in the box to complete the word.
   (Remember the *k* or *ck* Spelling Rule.)

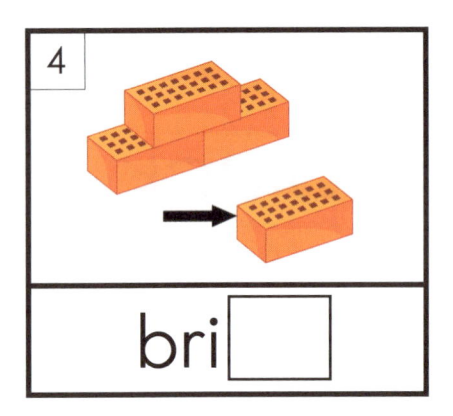

1. mas[k]
2. du[ck]
3. sin[k]
4. bri[ck]
5. li[ck]
6. des[k]
7. clo[ck]
8. mil[k]
9. tru[ck]

POP WORDS

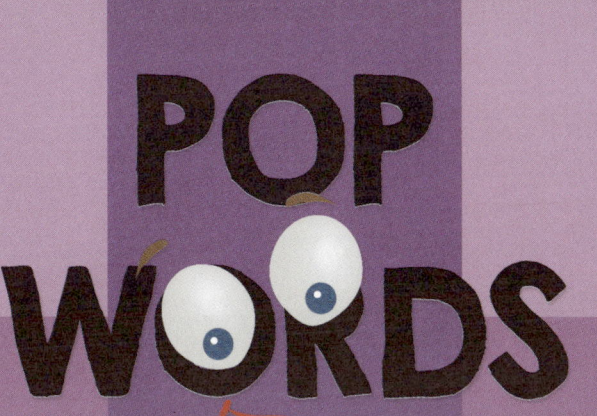

Note: The following two pages show all of the pop words covered in this book. They are listed by column in the order they were taught. Most of these words are high frequency words that could not be completely sounded out at the time when they were introduced.

a	you	me	so
the	to	she	her
is	do	be	said
on	his	we	as
I	down	off	this
have	for	are	that
of	went	all	with
and	was	no	they
has	he	go	by

POP WORDS

from	see	blue	like
my	look	brown	out
what	were	green	into
when	some	orange	first
which	one	pink	now
how	two	purple	come
or	more	red	these
your	color	white	other
	black	yellow	many

High Frequency Words

The following two pages show high frequency words that can be read phonetically at this point. They are listed on this page by column in the order of the phonetic scope and sequence of this book.

am	in	tell	best
an	it	well	fast
at	sit	will	help
can	not	call	jump
had	but	back	just
man	run	wish	must
ran	up	them	sing
big	us	then	thing
did	get	much	think
him	let	such	thank
if	yes	stop	called
	its	ask	

High Frequency Words

These high-frequency words are the same as those listed on the previous page. They are listed here in a random order for additional practice.

in	get	sing	at
us	stop	wish	it
am	man	well	up
tell	best	then	ran
big	think	such	yes
just	jump	thank	will
not	called	back	him
ask	much	help	but
did	them	thing	sit
its	fast	must	let
an	had	call	if
	run	can	